TERRY TAN'S
Straits Chinese Cookbook

TERRY TAN'S
Straits Chinese Cookbook

Times Books International
Singapore • Kuala Lumpur

© **1989 Times Books International**
Times Centre, 1 New Industrial Road
Singapore 1953
2nd Floor, Wisma Hong Leong Yamaha,
50 Jalan Pencala, 46050 Selangor Darul Ehsan
Malaysia

First published 1981
Reprinted 1988

Printed by Kim Hup Lee Printing Co. Pte. Ltd.

ISBN 9971 65 523 3

To Dot and Chris,
for whom I cook with love

Foreword

When our Company commenced packing spices in small bottles for the retail consumer market we were requested by our distributors overseas to supply those spices which are relatively unknown outside of Southeast Asia and which are not produced by our competitors. These 'exotic' spices as we have termed them include *serai* (lemon grass), *lengkuas* (galingale), *pandan* (screw pine), laksa leaves (*daun kesom*), curry leaves, etc., without which the preparation of traditional Southeast Asian cuisine is impossible. Our distributors requested these items for their Asian customers living overseas who wanted the taste of genuine home cooking.

At first, procuring the raw materials from the smallholders in Singapore was simple but as more and more of the farms were bulldozed to make way for the rapid urbanisation and industrialisation of the island, and as demand increased, it became necessary for the Company to embark on its own spice farm project in Malaysia.

It came as a surprise that when the bottled 'exotic' spices were first offered for sale in the supermarkets and grocery shops in Singapore, they proved extremely popular, but then it was realised that the same bulldozers which deprived the company of its source of raw materials also deprived the Singapore housewife of her fresh ingredients!

We had been fans of Terry Tan's *Sunday Nation* articles 'Cooking with Love' and 'Table for One' for some time and one Sunday we noted a glaring omission from one of his recipes. We contacted him personally and when asked why he had missed out that particular ingredient, he replied, 'because you cannot buy it in the local market any more'. He was not aware that we had been bottling that and the other exotic spices for some time.

One thing led to another. Being a purist, he scorned the use of bottled spices but conceded that being now in the age of convenience foods and the working housewife, one has to approach cooking more pragmatically. Terry agreed to experiment with ground spices and in his subsequent recipes, published in the *Sunday Nation*, dispelled once and for all the myth that ground spices are no substitute for fresh spices.

During our association with Terry, quite apart from his obvious culinary talent, his wealth of knowledge and experience of Peranakan cooking slowly revealed itself, and it became obvious to everyone that he has a great knowledge of not only Peranakan cooking but all Southeast Asian cooking.

With its unique mixture of eastern and western cultures, it is only natural that the best of both worlds is manifest in Singaporean cuisine in general and Peranakan cooking in particular. With the encroachment of the hamburger and hot dog it became essential that the art of Singaporean cooking be preserved in written form before the knowledge is lost forever. We are all fortunate therefore that we were able to prevail on Terry to record his encyclopedic knowledge for posterity. This is not 'just another cookbook' but will in time be acknowledged as the standard reference book of Peranakan cooking and will take its rightful place on the food lover's bookshelf along with Mrs Beeton and Larousse.

Michael Sweet
Spices of the Orient

Preface

When I entertain my friends, the first question they are apt to ask is the inevitable 'Did you learn to cook at a school?' Far from protesting vehemently that I was self-taught, I must admit I did learn my cooking at the best of schools.

It was a school established long before I was even born, a school that had no gleaming work tops or sophisticated equipment. No clanging bell was needed to summon students to be seated and agonise through the lessons. My classroom was the capacious family kitchen (my grandparents and different uncles and aunts all lived in rambling houses which I stayed in during school holidays from time to time), the hub of family activity. Warm smells of roasting *belacan* (a prawn paste) and eye-stinging fumes from simmering curries on wood-burning stoves beckoned us from the most protracted play outside.

It has been my greatest privilege to have been born into a family where there were any number of relatives who were superb cooks. But more than anyone else, it was my mother who gave me the best lessons in culinary arts. For nigh on twenty-five years before she passed on, I helped her cook, learning all the time without realising it.

My sisters were all married by the time I was nine and father having died the year before, it fell on me and my two brothers to help with the household chores. Though we had family retainers who had been with us for more than thirty years, they were by then too feeble to do much more than babysit.

Each of us would do one chore and the task of peeling onions, beating eggs and pounding chillies usually fell on me. Since I was the youngest (and the smallest in build) I was naturally the victim of elder sibling bullying. On reflection, I can only thank my family for subjecting me to all the endless grinding for I was really into the great university of cooking. There was never any conscious effort on my part to learn cooking—at least before I reached the age of reason and logic and because pounding onions endlessly was hateful— but it was the best way to learn. My mother, like her mother before her, never wrote anything down, committing every recipe she knew to memory. This may seem a prodigious task, knowing, as she did, some hundreds of ways to cook chicken, pork, fish or vegetables, but what choice had she? She never went to school and could not even read the numerals from one to ten. It was sometime around the mid-fifties that I realised all these recipes would be lost if someone did not record them. I guess I must have seemed odd to be jotting down how many onions went into Itek Sio and how many tablespoons of coriander were needed for curry when others of my generation were playing with tops and kites! I was no more than 14 then.

I am also grateful for the fact that, after my father died, we had to keep ourselves alive by renting out rooms in our rambling house to bachelor teachers from Taiping, Ipoh and Penang. So the cooking started in greater measure. For close on ten years I was the family's chef, preparing huge meals for sometimes twelve people. I hated it at first, what with having to study my Shakespeare and Durell's mathematics at the same time, but it answers my friends' question, how I learnt to cook.

As any Nonya or Baba cook will tell you, the skill to *agak* (approximate) is the hallmark of every good cook—which accounts for the fact that there are so few books on good Nonya home cooking.

Many friends have lamented that we have no Nonya food restaurants to speak of. There is good reason for this. Nonya food does not lend itself well to bulk cooking and most of the delicate curries and sambals must be prepared minutes before they are to be eaten. Though bottled herbs and spices, even of such rarities as laksa leaves, are now easily available (see Spices—Fresh or Bottled, p. 22) and curry pastes can be made in a jiffy, lovers of Nonya food tend to be the most critical of all gourmets, the common criticism being 'not nice, you must eat my aunt Lucy's laksa'.

Herein lies the greatest tribute to Nonya cooking. Each exponent of it has great pride in his or her family recipes and there are still families today who make a great feast of it every weekend when they gather together to chop, grind and simmer up great pots of the most redolent Nonya curries, soups and stews. You can do the same with the help of this book.

Acknowledgements

Special thanks to Andrew Merewether who put more beauty in my dishes with his camera than I did with my ladle, C. K. Tang and Aw Pottery for the loan of their crockery and utensils, C.K. Tseng for his stunning antiques, and last but not least, my mother-in-law Mdm Chay May Lin and sister-in-law Alice Tan for their unstinting help in the kitchen.

Contents

Foreword by Michael Sweet 6
Preface 8
Acknowledgements 9
Useful Hints 14
Spices—Fresh or Bottled? 22
Weights and Measures 23

Fish and Other Seafood

Ikan Parang Tempera 25
Fish in Tamarind and Soy Sauce 26
Ikan Goreng Asam 26
Sambal Lengkong 26
Ikan Garam Asam 27
Ikan Jebong Goreng Taucheo 27
Fish Moolie 28
Terry's Fish Curry in Lemon Juice 28
Ikan Parang Asam Pedas 33
Acar Ikan 33
Ikan Otak Otak 34
Fish Curry with Salted Vegetable 35
Ikan Kuah Lada 35
Ikan Panggang with Sambal Kicap 36
Steamed Ikan Kekek 36
Ikan Kekek Goreng Taucheo 36
Fried Fish with Dried Prawn
  Sambal 37
Baby Shark Curry with Lady's
  Fingers 37
Whole Pomfret with Sambal 38
Sembilang Masak Pedas 38
Sweet-Sour Garoupa 39
Ikan Masak Asam Pekat 39
Tenggiri in Hot Bean Paste 40
Hot Fish Curry 40
Tamban Goreng Asam 45
Fish Stuffed with Turmeric and
  Chilli 45
Steamed Ikan Bilis with Taucheo
  and Chilli 45
Sambal Udang Belimbing 46
Prawn Compote 46
Hot Sambal Goreng 47
Salt and Pepper Prawns 47
Udang Goreng Chilli 47
Sambal Grago 48
Prawns Stuffed with Sambal 48

Prawns with Kangkung 48
Udang Goreng Asam 49
Crunchy Prawn Curry 49
Udang Lobok Goreng Taucheo 49
Kepeting Bakar 50
Bakwan Kepeting 50
Crab Fried with Taucheo and Chilli 51
Sotong Goreng Chilli 51
Kepah Goreng 51
Siput Lemak 52

Pork, Beef and Mutton

Babi Hong 54
Pork, Cucumber and Egg Drop
  Soup 54
Deep-fried Meatballs in Pig's Caul 55
Hati Babi Bungkus 55
Soybean Cakes Stuffed with Spicy
  Minced Pork 56
Lemak Bittergourd Stuffed with
  Minced Pork 56
Tauyu Bak with Tau Pok 57
Fried Pork with Liver and Onions 57
Spiced Roast Pork 58
Babi Pong Teh 58
Pork Tempera 59
Pork with Pineapple and Green
  Chillies 59
Lor Bak 60
Fried Pepper Pork 60
Opor Babi 65
Babi Chin 65

Lemon Pork 66
Fried Asam Pork 66
Sambal Goreng Babi 66
Pork à la Shiok 67
Dry Pork Curry 67
Pork Curry 68
Rebong Lemak with Pork Ribs 68
Satay Babi Goreng 69
Teehee Char Rebong 69
Pork Ribs with Buah Keluak 70
Beef Rendang 70
Fried Minced Beef with Kiam Chye
  and Tomato 71
Hot Beef Curry 71
Beef Satay 72
Satay Gravy 72
Mutton Rendang 73

Poultry

Deep-fried Chicken 74
Ayam Bakar with Chilli 75
Grilled Spiced Spring Chicken 75
Fried Chicken with Ginger and
  Pepper 76
Ayam Lemak Putih 76
Chicken and Bamboo Shoot Curry 77
Chicken Kurmah 77
Roast Chicken in Coconut Milk 78
Chicken Tempera 78
Spicy Fried Chicken 79
Chicken Liver with Pineapple 79
Chicken Curry 79
Itek Sio 80

Vegetables

An Ulam Meal 85
Jaganan 87
Angled Loofah, Carrot and Egg
  Omelette 88
Hot Vegetable Curry 88
Long Beans in Dry Spices 89
Nangka Lemak 89
Egg and Kiam Chye Omelette 90
Brinjals with Sambal Udang Kering 90
Fried Chye Poh and Long Bean
  Sambal 91
Lady's Fingers with Prawn
  Sambal 91
Koo Chye Flowers with Taukwa 92
Sayur Lodeh 92
Lontong Rice Cakes 93
Vegetable Lemak with Sweet
  Potatoes 93
Homemade Rojak 94
Jantong Pisang 95

Sambals and Special Dishes

Yong Taufu Lemak 97
Acar 98
Cucumber Pickle 99
Sambal Kuakchye 99
Quick Saltfish Sambal 99
Saltfish Pickle 100
Sambal Telur 100
Sambal Bendi Santan 105

Leeks Fried with Prawns 105
Chilli Padi Sauce with Lime 106
Kacang Goreng 106
Fried Ikan Bilis with Peanuts in
  Chilli 107
Pineapple Sambal with Belacan 107
Sambal Nenas 108
Sambal Serondeng 108
Mango Sambal 108
Nasi Lemak with Lauk Piring 109
Ikan Pari Masak Pedas 109
Kangkung Lemak 110
Telur Goreng 110
Sambal Babi with Chin Char Loke 110
Pork Skin and Cucumber Sambal 111
Popiah 111

Oodles of Noodles

Mee Sua with Kidney and Liver
  Soup 117
Nonya Mee 118
Fried Bee Hoon with Cabbage 119
Mee Goreng Terry 119
Mee Siam 120
Sweet Noodles with Hardboiled
  Eggs 121

Rice and All Things Nice

Fried Rice Orient 122
Nasi Ulam 123

Fried Rice Shanghai Style 123
Nasi Biryani with Chicken 124
Nasi Goreng Nya Bulat 125

Soups of the Nonyas

Stuffed Cuttlefish Soup 126
Chicken and Macaroni Soup 127
Cucumber and Egg Drop Soup 127
Pong Tauhu Soup 128
Radish and Dried Cuttlefish Soup 128
Bee Tai Mak Soup 129
Tauhu Titiek 129
Chap Chye Soup 130
Hee Peow Soup 130
Itek Tim 131

My Teochew, Hokkien and Cantonese Heritage

Terry's Chicken Stew 137
Bak Kng 137
Fried Hokkien Mee 138
Taukwa Goreng Chye Poh 138
Hokkien Mee Soup 139
Chicken, Mushroom and Quail's
   Egg Soup 139
Saltfish Rice in Clay Pot 140
Winter Melon Soup with Chicken 140
Chicken in Soy Sauce 141
Sweetcorn and Chicken Soup 141
Stewed Chicken Wings 142

Braised Duck with Chestnuts,
   Dried Oysters and Liver Stuffing 143
Fish Head and Bee Hoon Soup 144

Kuih-Kuih

Steamed Tapioca with Grated
   Coconut and Sugar 145
Kuih Bangkit 146
Tapioca Squares in Grated
   Coconut 146
Pengat 147
Onde Onde 147
Pulot Hitam 148
Kuih Wajek 148
Kuih Keria 149
Green Beans in Coconut Milk 149
Kuih Lapis 150
Sweet Potato and Ginger Dessert 150
Kuih Pisang 151
Sago Pudding with Gula Melaka 151
Kuih Dada 152
Pengat Pisang Rajah 152
Kuih Jongkong 157
Kuih Bengka Ubi Kayu 158
Agar-Agar Santan 158
Steamed Serikaya 159
Pulot Serikaya 160
Homemade Tau Hwey Chui 161

Glossary 162
Curriculum Vitae 168
Index 169

Useful Hints

Almonds

Going on the premise that half a loaf is better than none, keep a small amount of almonds at ready as they make decent substitutes for candlenuts (*buah keras*). This latter, because of its rich oil content, has not been processed into ground form and bottled. As for keeping whole candlenuts, it's a devilishly difficult job because they are prone to infestation by mealybugs. At best, you can refrigerate them in an airtight bottle but even this does not prevent them from going 'off' after a few weeks. Candlenuts are invaluable in many Nonya dishes which use *rempah* that needs sweetness and thickness. Skinned and ground almonds come close to doing this job.

Bamboo Shoots

As a converted purist, I see little reason to slave for hours over fresh bamboo shoots, which are not only troublesome to prepare but hard to come by, when canned bamboo shoots do as well. Canned bamboo keeps very well indefinitely in their cans when opened, up to three weeks immersed in water in the refrigerator. As a vegetable that adds bulk, and the star ingredient in Popiah and Rebong Lemak, bamboo is unsurpassable. It also has a remarkable versatility in blending with many meats and other vegetables.

Buah Keluak

This is, undeniably, ambrosia among Nonya dishes, but like the durian it calls for an acquired taste. To the uninitiated, *buah keluak* is a black nut from Indonesia about the size of a misshapen golf ball. The surface is ridged with a smooth nut 'mouth' across the flattest part. A slit is made in this mouth through which one scrapes out the contents which has been variously described as 'opium' and 'soft tar'. The taste is indescribable and has to be eaten to be believed. Good nuts, when cooked, should be richly black and oily. To prepare *buah keluak*, wash and scrub thoroughly until the thin film of dried mud they come in is completely gone. This has to be a proper job if you do not want reconstituted mud in your *keluak* gravy. Soak in a large pot of water overnight or for at least six hours. An even quicker method is to boil the *keluak* for 15 minutes, which, I'm told by friends, works just as well.

Candlenuts (*Buah Keras*)

Buy only small amounts of this shelled, creamy-white nut as they don't keep well. Buying them unshelled entails the bother of cracking them open which is a troublesome job. (See ALMONDS.)

Coconut Milk

What would we do without this beautiful ingredient? Though there are canned coconut creams and desiccated coconut on the market which can be used with almost as much efficacy as real coconut milk, they are not nearly as *lemak*. This, perhaps more than any other word in Nonya cuisine, is the catchall word that sums up taste, flavour and bouquet. You often see recipes that call for grated coconut to be squeezed twice— once for first milk and the second time for thinner milk. You are also not told why. There is no mystique here. Rich first milk is added last because, in slow-simmering curries, the process can render too much oil from the milk. Unless you are cooking some dish that requires no less than an hour of simmering, do not bother with this two-step process. Coconut milk, with a pinch of salt added, can be frozen and kept for up to a week. There is not much point in using a substitute as fresh coconut is so easy to come by, praise be for well-organised markets.

Curry Powder

There is no mystique in curry powders or pastes. Each cook has his blend of spices; whether it contains more or less of one or the other ingredient is a matter of individual taste. The spices used are generally unvarying except for ingredients like onions, ginger and whole spices. There are so many brands of ready-mixed curry powders in the market that make cooking curry so much easier today, unlike in our mothers' days when each blend had to be specially mixed. Spices of the Orient has the entire range of curry powders that can be kept indefinitely with no danger of mealybugs spoiling them because they are all sterilised. However, if you wish to make your own, here are some blending suggestions.

Meat Curry Powder
400 g ground coriander
150 g ground aniseed
100 g ground cummin
100 g black or white pepper
150 g chilli powder
80 g ground turmeric
2 cinnamon sticks, about 5 cm long } ground separately
10 g cardamoms
8 cloves

Fish Curry Powder
400 g ground coriander
150 g ground aniseed
150 g ground cummin
100 g black or white pepper
150 g chilli powder
70 g ground turmeric
10 cardamoms
6 star anise } ground separately
6 cloves
2 cinnamon sticks, about 5 cm long
40 g fenugreek, left whole

Mix spices well and store in airtight bottles. To make paste, add water or cooking liquid in the proportion 2 tablespoons liquid to 1 tablespoon curry powder.

Daun Limau Purut

Never before has there been a herb with such a vile name and such magnificent flavour. *Daun limau purut*, sometimes called the leaf of the leprous lime on account of the fruit's gnarled skin, is without question the maharajah of herbs. I grew up on it, thrived on it and would not go without it for longer than a week at a stretch. It has a fragrance that haunts without overpowering. It goes into just about every lemon grass based dish and takes over in such a subtle way you hardly know it's there. Yet, without *daun limau purut*, the classic *Satay Babi Goreng* would be a pale shadow of itself.

There are two varieties. One is small, about 4 cm long and shaped like a guitar. The other is large, about the size of a child's palm and just as fragrant. Both originate from Thailand. One leaf, shredded, goes a long way and if you are buying to store, keep them in dry plastic bags and freeze. Very hard to come by.

Ginger

When using ginger as one of the ingredients to be pounded, it is better to use the common light brown root ginger which is sold by dry goods stalls in markets. For using as garnish and in steamed dishes, use young ginger sold by vegetable vendors. This is pale yellow with green tinges where the stalks begin.

Kwali (Wok)

This is an item you cannot do without. Yet, strange to say, few supermarkets sell them. Most HDB markets have stalls selling them. Frying, stewing, steaming and just about every method of cooking can be done with a *kwali*. The best type is still the black cast-iron one with two handles, though I find the new non-stick *kwali* excellent for slow braising. The cast-iron *kwali* do not come with lids but any tight-fitting aluminium cover will do when you steam or braise. One virtually lasts forever if you don't drop it on the floor and crack it.

Pandan (Screwpine) Leaves

Pandan or screwpine leaves are indispensable to Nonya dishes, especially in desserts and steamed coconut rice. It has a subtle tang that bears no similarity to any manufactured essence. Possibly one of the easiest plants to grow in pots—even in a tin of water—they are also excellent as a source of green food colouring that comes with built-in flavour.

Pestle and Mortar or Electric Blender?

Both do the job of grinding spices just as well. It depends on how willing you are to compromise and dispel the myth that only age-old methods produce good results. If you are cooking for a few people, the pestle and mortar is handy. But when cooking for, say, 12 people, you would need to pound spices several times which is impractical and tedious. I have used the blender for *rempah* for anything from curries to *acar* and even *sambal belacan* and can honestly say taste is not compromised. Our mothers had all the time in the world to sit and pound for hours. We don't and a commonsense attitude towards using implements and bottled spices means you get to eat more dishes you would otherwise not bother to cook.

Rempah (Mixed Spices)

The importance of frying *rempah* (*tumis*) for cooking Nonya dishes cannot be emphasised enough. Whatever the mixture, the oil used must be fresh, the *kwali* hot and the heat low to medium. *Rempah* must be constantly stirred, with a to-and-fro motion that prevents it from sticking to the pan. If it does stick, sprinkle a little water or whatever cooking liquid you have at hand and lower heat. *Rempah* is only ready (for other ingredients to be put in) when oil seeps out again. Never ever try to cut time by adding other ingredients before this happens. You will only end up with a dish that has a 'raw' smell and your efforts wasted. For every recipe where the word *rempah* is mentioned, it means ingredients listed are to be ground or blended. Bottled ground ingredients are to be mixed in after grinding.

OPPOSITE: 1 Cinnamon, 2 Dried turmeric, 3 Black peppercorns, 4 Mustard seeds, 5 Whole nutmegs, 6 Curry powder, 7 Star anise, 8 Shallots, 9 Garlic, 10 Dried Chillies, 11 Mace, 12 Whole nutmegs, 13 Fresh red chillies, 14 Lime *(limau nipis)*, 15 *Chilli padi,* 16 Fresh green chillies, 17 Small limes *(limau kesturi),* 18 Cardamom, 19 Coriander.

Root spices like onions, garlic, ginger and lemon grass should be sliced to facilitate pounding. Dried chillies should be soaked in hot water to soften and wash any dust away before pounding. Chilli stalks should be removed. The order in which you put spices in to pound is not important, but onions are generally added last so the liquid does not spray all over you. Unless otherwise specified, spices are to be pounded fine.

Tok Panjang (Long Table of Food)

If there is anything I miss about the Straits Chinese traditions it's the *Tok Panjang* way of entertaining. This literally means Long Table, one on which a plethora of sambals, curries and soups would be laid and guests would take turns sitting down to help themselves. Unlike the buffet style of today, Nonyas and Babas then would not pile several different dishes onto their plates of rice. It was no way to enjoy such good food

as, in order to savour the subtle tanginess of one *asam* dish or the fiery chilli sambal of another, one would take as much as needed for a mouthful and eat it with rice.

There would be no shortage of helpers to replenish the dishes as diners emptied them. Rich families had several servants to do this and those not as affluent usually had many relatives who were willing helpers. Today, it is rare for any Straits Chinese family to serve food at a similar long table. The food may be the same but guests will pile everything onto their plates and do a terrible injustice to the cook by eating everything mixed beyond taste recognition!

The *Tok Panjang* also had traditional dishes that remained unchanged for many years. Typical ones were Bakwan Kepeting, Nonya Mee, Buah Keluak, Chicken Curry, Hee Peow Soup, Sambal Timun and Itek Sio. But whatever was served, there would always be enough *sambal belacan* for everyone.

PAGES 18-19: 1 Chicken Curry (recipe p. 79), 2 Itek Tim (recipe p. 131), 3 Bakwan Kepeting (recipe p. 50), 4 Sambal Belacan (recipe p. 86), 5 Hee Peow Soup (recipe p. 130), 6 Pork Skin and Cucumber Sambal (recipe p. 111), 7 Hati Babi Bungkus (recipe p. 55), 8 Nonya Mee (recipe p. 118), 9 Pork Ribs with Buah Keluak (recipe p. 70), 10 Satay Babi Goreng (recipe p. 69).

OPPOSITE: How to Serve an Ulam Meal (recipe pp. 85-87). Clockwise from top left: *buah petai,* cucumber, *kacang botol,* cabbage, *buah jering,* pounded dried prawns, chillies, *parang* (wolf herring), *chin char loke, sambal belacan.*

Spices – Fresh or Bottled?

I am the first to admit there is nothing to beat using fresh spices and herbs for Nonya cooking. But it is neither realistic nor helpful if I fiercely go on propounding this on the premise that there is no substitute. Most of us do not have the time nor the inclination to bother with the elaborate preparations required of Nonya cooking if you simply must use fresh spices and herbs.

My mother, when she was alive and saw my attempts to take short cuts in preparing spices (I hated it then), snorted that I would turn out garbage. As I grew older, it was still no use budging the old lady that my future wife wasn't going to spend hours grinding onions after spending eight hours at her office. Still less was she going to bother with selecting garlic cloves of exact size to go into *acar*.

I was never more glad than when pursuing the story of how Spices of the Orient had successfully bottled basic spices used in Nonya cooking. Up to then, most basic spices like coriander (*ketumbar*), turmeric (*kunyit*) and others used in western cooking were easily available. But when it came to things like lemon grass (*serai*), galingale (*lengkuas*), prawn paste (*belacan*), tamarind (*asam*) and laksa leaves (*daun kesom*), no one had bottled them for the supermarket shelf.

I have since found that using ground versions of practically every spice and herb used in Nonya cooking has not ruined my reputation or the taste in any way. Even the best of classic cooking has to bend to inevitable change. Lifestyles today do not permit time-consuming processes that, in any case, have much easier and, often, automated alternatives. It is largely a myth that onions taste better when pounded in the stone pestle and mortar (*batu lesong*). I rarely use this method today except for preparing small amounts which dragging out the blender for is too much of a chore.

But as any cook will agree, a blender or food processor is a great boon. If you do any cooking on a regular basis, *sambal* pastes can be made in bulk and frozen for later use. Most fresh spices do not keep well in any case. Ground spices, if sterilised and kept in airtight bottles, keep indefinitely.

It is also through Spices of the Orient that this book has been made possible. It was my meeting with the two directors of the company, Mr Michael Sweet and Miss Julie Yeo, that sparked off the discussion which led to this, my contribution to the Straits-born heritage. I thank both Miss Yeo and Mr Sweet in not only having faith in my skills as a cook but for loving Nonya food to distraction. I have also worked these past 12 months on this book in the belief that taking short cuts like using ground spices can only help to perpetuate Nonya cuisine, the preparation of which would normally scare novice cooks away.

It is only when a certain dish demands one or several fresh herbs, like bruised lemon grass or sliced galingale, that I use them. In these cases, using ground spices would alter the taste too much. Few will argue with this, for in dishes like Garam Asam (fish in tamarind liquid), a stalk of fresh, bruised lemon grass not only enhances the flavour but also the presentation.

For sheer convenience, when you have a sudden passion for a curry and fresh spices are just not available, bottled ones are hard to beat. I have cooked Laksa with tinned coconut cream, dried spices and even ground laksa leaves (*daun kesom*) for dinner, and friends, far from being critical, admired my ingenuity. It is not ingenuity, but the willingness to adapt to a renaissance in cooking.

This is also no reflection on my friends' culinary skills but a compliment to them for being true modernists in thought and gourmets in taste. As a last word, Nonya cooking can be tedious in preparation if you are anything less than the skilled cooks my mother and aunts were. There is an easier, far better way so that recipes can be shared by all and the beautiful tradition of Nonya cooking handed down.

I sincerely hope you will find many hours of pleasure trying out recipes in this book, as much as I have enjoyed trying them out. For the novice cooks, whatever may be lacking in your finished dish, it will have been more than made up for with the love that went into it. This last is another reason for this book. I love nothing more than cooking dishes for, and sharing with, my family.

Weights and Measures

Though we are still grappling with the mysteries of the metric system, I find it by far the easiest method once attuned to it. It is worthwhile to remember—and reduce the mystery a little—that in most Nonya dishes, the exact amount of water used is not *de rigueur.* This is not to say you can add any amount you want but a give-or-take of 30 or 40 millilitres for gravy dishes will not ruin your dish beyond recognition. Take comfort in knowing that our grandmothers never bothered with exact measurements anyway.

Mass Weights

15 g	½ oz
30 g	1 oz
50 g	1 ¾ oz
100 g	3 ½ oz
250 g	8 oz (½ lb)
500 g	1 lb
1 kg	2 lbs

METRIC	IMPERIAL	CUP	US
80 ml	3 fl oz	½ cup	¼ pint
150 ml	5 fl oz	⅔ cup	¼ pint (imp)
250 ml	10 fl oz	1 ¼ cups	½ pint (imp)
500 ml	20 fl oz	2 ½ cups	1 pint

Fish and Other Seafood

The fondest memories of my childhood are of the balmy days (and nights) I spent in my grandparents' home, a sprawling house facing the sea at Siglap. The sea is no more there, in its place towering blocks built by the Housing and Development Board, and I feel a great sadness that my son will never spend idyllic days romping by the shore hunting for shells and hermit crabs. What could be more exciting for a nine-year-old than diving from a *sampan* into shallow water off a sandbank?

Though the old house was large, a copy of a similar one in Swatow, China, where my great-grandfather lived before migrating here, the kitchen was rather cramped, but adjoining the kitchen was this great open area where stood my grandmother's favourite grinding implements. Her *batu giling* was a large slab of hewn granite and the roller needed much strength to be lifted. She would use this to grind a lot of spices when there were meals to be cooked for 20 people, but used her smaller *batu lesong* (pestle and mortar) when cooking a smaller amount.

Whatever she and my aunts cooked, and however little or much, it was always mouth-watering. Sometimes my mother would help. When we visited she would make a beeline for the beach where, come drizzle or fierce sun, she would spend hours scraping at the damp sand for *remis* (bean clam). This is a small mollusc that she would gather buckets of at the end of the day to pickle in soy sauce and chilli. I have not eaten this for nearly 15 years and you can rarely find *remis* anywhere today.

There was always fish on the table. Fish, fresh and leaping just minutes ago, still wet-eyed and breathing furiously in the holds of *sampans*. As a city boy in my later years, I never could wake up to see the sunrise but here, at my grandmother's house by the sea, sleep was the last thing I wanted. At the crack of dawn I would be up in my pair of ragged shorts and singlet (tee-shirts were a decade away) to see the fishermen bring in their catch. What a sight! *Sampans* for two, five, eight or twelve, they came crunching onto the shore and many Kampung Siglap folk would be waiting, with money in hand, to buy the *ikan parang* (wolf herring), baskets of tiny shrimps and cuttlefish for prices you wouldn't believe today.

The *kuah lada* (literally, chilli-hot gravy) my grandmother cooked with catfish or ray fish is the tastiest I have eaten, then or now. (If there is anything I will argue till the cows come home, it is the difference fresh fish makes to a dish. Never mind what achievements refrigeration has made in perpetuating the belief that fish frozen at the right moment will retain all its freshness.) Tiny shrimps would be made into *chin char loke*, a pickled delicacy eaten with chillies, shallots, lime juice and even the lime skin. And with a side of fried *parang*, it made a meal I gladly left my swimming for.

Sometimes, tiny cuttlefish would be so abundant, some kind fisherman would give us kids a scoop at no cost and we would rush to the kampung *chai tau kway* (radish rice cake) man and persuade him to fry it with 20 cents of his delicious rice cakes in sweet sauce. He would grumble that the cuttlefish ink made his pan black but usually relented when we told him his pan was black anyway. My mouth waters still when I think of this heavenly breakfast.

But undeniably one of the best ways to eat fish then was up on a *kelong*. This fishing stake was where the catches came from and we would often follow the fisherman to his grounds and stay awake all night helping winch up his net. Whatever he could not get into his large wooden boxes used to store fish until the early morning, he would steam on a makeshift stove. *Ikan bilis* (anchovy), prawns and crabs were chucked into his huge *kwali* and steamed without even being washed first. We ate them innocent of all but a sprinkle of salt.

Those were the halcyon days when my mother learnt a great deal more about cooking fish the Straitsborn way. As a young girl she had learnt from her mother, but being married off at 17, there was much she did not know. Each time we stayed for the school holidays, she would learn a few more dishes and cook them when we came back to town. I think I learnt as much watching her, helping her skin and gut seafood, and being official taster whenever she wasn't sure if a dish was too hot or not salty enough. Nine times out of ten, her balance of taste was perfect. The *agak-agak* system of cooking is a skill that can only be learnt after years of practice. As much as I learnt how to cook, I learnt how to choose fresh fish, look for the best crabs and know which spices went with which type of fish best. There are compromises today because of changed lifestyles but they are compromises that do not necessarily rob a dish of its flavour. Then hours would be spent chopping, grinding and pounding spices for many dishes on weekends. Few have time for this today and bottled spices are a boon.

Ikan Parang Tempera

Cooking time: 12 minutes

2 pieces *parang* (wolf herring)
4 tablespoons oil
1 teaspoon *belacan* powder
1 tablespoon black soy sauce
1 teaspoon fish sauce
1 tablespoon vinegar
1 lime to be squeezed for juice
2 tablespoons sugar
300 millilitres water
1 large onion

Ingredients to be Sliced
2 stalks lemon grass
4 red chillies
3 cloves garlic
4 shallots
3 *daun limau purut*

Fry fish in oil for 6 minutes until cooked. Scoop out oil, leaving 2 tablespoons. Fry all sliced ingredients for 2 minutes, then add all other ingredients. When it boils, lower heat and put fish in to steep for a further 2 minutes. Serve garnished with onion sliced into rings.

Fish in Tamarind and Soy Sauce

Cooking time: 15 minutes

500 g *selangat* **(gizzard shad, Cantonese:** *wong yee*)
1.5 litres water
5 tablespoons tamarind powder
3 tablespoons black soy sauce
2 limes
1 teaspoon salt
1 teaspoon pepper
1 teaspoon monosodium glutamate

Wash and clean fish thoroughly. Boil all ingredients and add fish to simmer for 15 minutes. This fish is meant to be cooked until its bones are soft and edible. Gravy goes well with plain rice.

Ikan Goreng Asam

Cooking time: 10 minutes

6 pieces *tenggiri* **(Spanish mackerel)**
3 tablespoons fresh tamarind paste
275 millilitres water } *combined*
1 tablespoon black soy sauce
4 tablespoons oil
1 tablespoon black soy sauce
2 red chillies, sliced

Marinate fish in asam and sauce mixture for 30 minutes. Drain but do not wash. Deep-fry in hot oil for 6 minutes. Serve with a side dip of black soy sauce and sliced red chillies.

Sambal Lengkong

Cooking time: 1 hour

2 whole *parang* **(wolf herring)**
2 coconuts, grated
300 millilitres water
2 teaspoons salt
4 tablespoons sugar

Rempah
20 dried chillies
4 *chilli padi* **(bird chillies)**
20 shallots
10 candlenuts
1 teaspoon ground turmeric
2 tablespoons *belacan* **powder**
1 tablespoon lemon grass powder

Cut *parang* into wedges and steam for 10 minutes. When cool, flake meat carefully and remove all bones. Pound flaked fish meat using pestle and mortar. Leave aside. Squeeze coconuts with water for thick milk.

In a *kwali*, preferably non-stick, add all ingredients and stir-fry for about 1 hour until fish is dry and crisp. This is a laborious dish to cook but the results are well worth the effort. Sambal Lengkong can be kept in jars for a week if the lid is tight-fitting.

Ikan Garam Asam

Cooking time: 15 minutes

5 tablespoons oil
3 tablespoons tamarind powder
800 millilitres water
600 g *tenggiri* **(Spanish mackerel)**
6 *belimbing buloh* **(sour star fruit)**
1 teaspoon salt
2 teaspoons sugar
1 stalk lemon grass, bruised

Rempah (pounded coarsely)
1 stalk lemon grass
4 candlenuts
4 red chillies
2 large onions
1 teaspoon ground turmeric
1 tablespoon galingale powder
1 tablespoon *belacan* **powder**

If you have an earthenware pot or *belangah* it makes an ideal pot for this dish. Don't use a metal pot for any dish cooked in asam. Chemical action turns the metal black and gives the gravy a 'metallic' taste.

Heat oil and fry *rempah* until fragrant. Add tamarind powder mixed with water and bring to a boil. While gravy is simmering, slice *tenggiri* into 2 cm thick pieces. Cut pith from *belimbing buloh* and halve each fruit. Add fish, *belimbing buloh*, salt, sugar and whole lemon grass and simmer for 8 minutes.

Ikan Jebong Goreng Taucheo

Cooking time: 10 minutes

Of all the denizens of the deep that I have eaten, few match this peculiar fish in taste and texture. The Malays call it ayam laut *or chicken of the sea as the meat tastes rather more like chicken than fish! It has an extremely tough skin which accounts for its English name—leatherjacket. I used to hate it when my mother bought* jebong *as it was my chore to remove the skin. It is so abrasive it can cause sore palms, especially if you have to skin some dozens of them.*

6 *jebong* **(leatherjacket)**
3 tablespoons oil
2 cloves garlic, crushed
3 slices ginger, cut into fine strips
2 red chillies, sliced
2 tablespoons preserved soy beans
(Hokkien: *taucheo***), washed and**
mashed lightly
275 millilitres water
1 teaspoon sugar
1 bunch spring onions, chopped

Clean *jebong* and leave whole as the head has the most tasty meat.

Heat oil and fry crushed garlic and ginger till light brown. Add sliced chillies and fry for 15 seconds. Add preserved soy beans and fry for 1 minute. Put *jebong* in (if fish are large, cut in two) and fry well for 1 minute. Add water and sugar and simmer for 5 minutes. Garnish with spring onions.

Fish Moolie

Cooking time: 15 minutes

1 *ikan merah* (red snapper),
   about 600 g
1 teaspoon salt
1 coconut, grated
300 millilitres water
8 tablespoons oil
1 teaspoon salt
1 teaspoon fish sauce
2 *daun limau purut*
2 tomatoes, quartered

Rempah
3 cm piece ginger, about 3 cm thick
2 large onions
1 teaspoon ground turmeric
2 tablespoons ground coriander
1 teaspoon ground cummin
1 tablespoon chilli powder

Clean and gut fish and rub with salt. Knead coconut with water for milk. Set aside.

Heat oil and fry fish until brown. Remove all but 4 tablespoons oil and fry *rempah* until fragrant. Add coconut milk, salt, fish sauce and *daun limau purut* and bring to a boil. Simmer for about 10 minutes until gravy thickens a little.

Add whole fish and simmer for 5 minutes more. Add tomatoes in the last 3 minutes of cooking for they become soft and mushy when boiled too long. (Another good garnish is a sprinkle of laksa leaves.)

Terry's Fish Curry in Lemon Juice

Cooking time: 10 minutes

4 tablespoons oil
1 stalk lemon grass, bruised
1 turmeric leaf
1 tablespoon tamarind powder
800 millilitres water
1 lemon
4 pieces *kurau* (threadfin),
   about 500 g
2 *daun limau purut*
1 stalk *daun kesom*
1 *bunga siantan* (ginger flower),
   separated into whole leaves
1 teaspoon salt
1 teaspoon fish sauce
2 teaspoons sugar

Rempah (pounded coarsely)
1 large onion
2 cloves garlic
4 red chillies
2 slices ginger
3 candlenuts
2 teaspoons *belacan* powder
1 teaspoon lemon grass powder

Fry *rempah* in oil until fragrant and add bruised lemon grass and turmeric leaf. Stir-fry for a minute and add tamarind powder mixed with water. Squeeze in juice from lemon. Bring to a boil and add all other ingredients. Simmer for 6–8 minutes.

OPPOSITE: Whole Pomfret with Sambal (recipe p. 38).
PAGE 30: Fish Curry with Salted Vegetable (recipe p. 35).

Ikan Parang Asam Pedas

Cooking time: 8 minutes

3 tablespoons tamarind powder
650 millilitres water
500 g *parang* (wolf herring)
1 teaspoon salt
1 teaspoon sugar
2 stalks lemon grass, bruised
2 green chillies
1 piece pineapple, sliced

Rempah
2 red chillies
1 cm piece turmeric
1 large onion
1 stalk lemon grass
1 teaspoon *belacan* powder
1 tablespoon galingale powder

Mix tamarind powder with water and bring to a boil. Add *rempah* and simmer for 2 minutes. Cut *parang* into two pieces and add to gravy. Add salt, sugar, whole lemon grass and green chillies, either left whole or sliced into two. Simmer for 5 minutes and add pineapple.

Acar Ikan

Cooking time: 20 minutes

500 g *kurau* (threadfin) fillet
1 teaspoon salt
1 teaspoon ground turmeric
5 tablespoons oil
500 millilitres vinegar
1 cucumber, quartered lengthwise,
    seeded, and cut into 3 cm lengths
1 carrot, cut into 3 cm lengths,
    ½ cm thick
1 large onion, quartered
2 green chillies, seeded
2 red chillies, seeded
6 shallots, peeled and left whole
1 tablespoon sugar
1 teaspoon salt
150 millilitres water

Rempah
1 large onion
3 cloves garlic
2 cm piece turmeric
1 small knob ginger, the size
    of a walnut
4 dried chillies, soaked in
    water till soft

Rub *kurau* fillet with salt and ground turmeric and fry in oil till golden brown. Leave aside.

Boil vinegar and scald all vegetables (from cucumber to shallots), a little at a time. Drain and squeeze out moisture.

In the oil left after frying fish, fry *rempah* till fragrant. Add sugar and salt and fry for another minute until sugar dissolves. Add water and simmer for a few minutes. Add scalded vegetables and stir once. Spoon *acar* over fried fish and serve.

PAGE 31: Ikan Otak Otak (recipe p. 34).
OPPOSITE: Ikan Kuah Lada (recipe p. 35).

Ikan Otak Otak

(Illustrated on p. 31)

Cooking time: 6–8 minutes

1 kg *tenggiri* **(Spanish mackerel) or fish meat**
2 coconuts, grated, for milk
300 millilitres water
½ coconut, skinned and grated
5 stalks *daun kesom***, sliced fine**
1 turmeric leaf, sliced fine
3 *daun limau purut***, sliced fine**
1 teaspoon salt
1 teaspoon sugar
4 eggs, beaten
2 tablespoons cornflour
20 pieces banana leaf, each 10 cm square

Rempah
8 candlenuts
4 large onions
15 dried chillies or 1 tablespoon chilli powder
2 tablespoons ground coriander
1 teaspoon ground turmeric
2 tablespoons *belacan* **powder**
1 tablespoon galingale powder
1 tablespoon lemon grass powder

If using fresh *tenggiri*, fillet fish and cut into slices. If using fish meat, shape into rectangular cakes 8 x 4 x 1 cm and soak in water. Prepared fish meat sold in markets tend to be salty.

Knead grated coconut with water for milk and leave aside. In a dry pan, fry skinned grated coconut until golden brown. Remove and pound till fine.

Mix *rempah* ingredients with coconut milk, sliced *kesom*, turmeric and *limau purut* leaves, salt, sugar, beaten eggs and cornflour. The consistency should be like soft butter.

Scald banana leaves in hot water to make them pliable. Put 2 heaped tablespoons of the mixture on each piece of banana leaf and make into parcels, securing by folding over at either side (see diagram). Grill in the oven or over hot coals for 6 minutes, turning once.

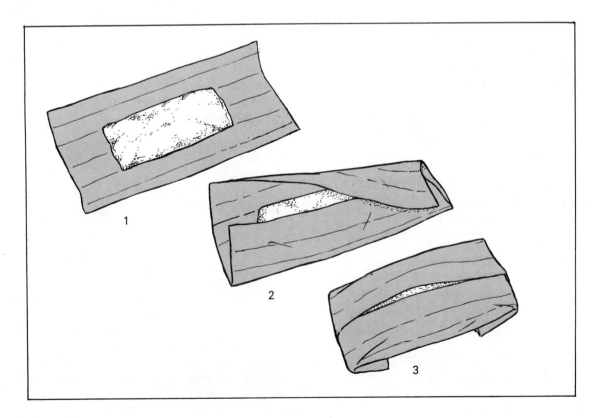

Fish Curry with Salted Vegetable

(Illustrated on p. 30)

Cooking time: 12 minutes

500 g *pari* (ray fish) or baby shark
3 tablespoons tamarind powder
850 millilitres water
150 g salted vegetable
   (Hokkien: *kiam chye*)
¼ coconut, grated
100 millilitres water
4 tablespoons oil
2 tablespoons fish curry powder
   (see p. 15)
1 tablespoon water
1 stalk curry leaves or 1 teaspoon
   curry leaf powder
1 stalk *bunga siantan* (wild ginger flower)
1 tablespoon sugar

Wash fish and cut into chunks. Mix tamarind powder with water. Wash salted vegetable and drain, squeezing it gently to rid it of some saltiness. Cut into large pieces. Squeeze grated coconut with 100 millilitres water for coconut milk.

Heat oil in *kwali* and fry curry powder that has been made into a paste with 1 tablespoon water until fragrant. Add salted vegetable and fry for 2 minutes more.

Add fish and fry for 1 minute until pieces are well coated. Add tamarind liquid, coconut milk, curry leaves and *bunga siantan* and bring to a boil. Simmer for 5 minutes and add sugar.

I have omitted salt in this dish as the vegetable is already salty. However, if your taste for salt is on the heavy side, add to taste.

Ikan Kuah Lada

(Illustrated on p. 32)

Cooking time: 9 minutes

500 g *tenggiri* (Spanish mackerel)
   or *pari* (ray fish)
2 brinjals
4 tablespoons oil
1 stalk lemon grass, bruised
4 tablespoons tamarind powder
700 millilitres water
1 teaspoon salt

Rempah

2 red chillies
4 candlenuts
2 cloves garlic
12 shallots
1 teaspoon ground turmeric
2 tablespoons black pepper
1 tablespoon galingale powder

Cut fish into large pieces. Halve brinjals lengthwise, remove stalk and make a cut right down two-thirds of each half.

Fry *rempah* in oil until fragrant. Add bruised lemon grass. Blend tamarind powder with water and add to spices. Bring to a boil and add fish and salt. Simmer for 2 minutes and add brinjals. Simmer for 5 minutes more and serve with *sambal belacan* (p. 86).

Ikan Panggang with Sambal Kicap

(Illustrated on p. 44)

Cooking time: 12 minutes

2 *bawal hitam* (black pomfret)
   or *selar* (yellowstripe trevally)
1 teaspoon salt
2 tablespoons oil

Sambal Kicap
4 tablespoons black soy sauce
1 tablespoon *sambal belacan* (p. 86)
2 limes
2 teaspoons sugar

Clean fish and rub with salt. Grill over char-coal or under oven grill for 5 minutes each side until skin is slightly charred. Baste with oil often. Keep warm.

Sambal Kicap
Mix soy sauce with *sambal belacan*. Squeeze juice of limes over it and mix well. Remove lime pith and slice skin into fine strips. Add to *sambal* with sugar and serve as a dip for grilled fish.

Steamed Ikan Kekek

Cooking time: 6–8 minutes

4 *kekek* (silver belly)
3 slices ginger, cut into strips
2 red chillies, cut into strips
6 strips pork fat (about 1
   tablespoonful)
2 tablespoons preserved soy beans,
   washed and drained

Score *kekek* with deep cuts on both sides. Put in a pyrex or steaming dish and spread all other ingredients well over fish. Steam for 6 minutes. When fish eyes pop out, they are cooked.

Ikan Kekek Goreng Taucheo

Cooking time: 8 minutes

4 tablespoons oil
2 cloves garlic, crushed
1 tablespoon preserved soy beans,
   mashed lightly
1 red chilli, sliced
1 teaspoon sugar
200 millilitres water
4 large *kekek* (silver belly),
   each cut into two
1 bunch Chinese parsley

Heat oil and fry garlic till brown. Add preserved soy beans and fry for 1 minute, then add chilli. Fry until mixture is fragrant, then add sugar. Add water and fish and simmer for 4 minutes. Serve with Chinese parsley.

Fried Fish with Dried Prawn Sambal

Cooking time: 20 minutes

4 heaped tablespoons dried prawns
hot water
6 *tenggiri* (Spanish mackerel)
    steaks
5 tablespoons oil
1 tablespoon water,
    to be used if necessary

Rempah
1 large onion
4 candlenuts
10 dried chillies, soaked in
    hot water
2 cloves garlic
1 tablespoon *belacan* powder
1 tablespoon galingale powder
1 teaspoon lemon grass powder
2 tablespoons sugar

Soak dried prawns in hot water for a few minutes then wash, drain and pound until fine.

Fry fish separately until pieces are light brown. Remove from oil and fry dried prawns for a few minutes. Add *rempah* and stir-fry over low heat for 10 minutes until oil seeps out again. Dried prawns tend to soak up oil alarmingly but do not add more oil. If mixture seems too dry add 1 tablespoon water for a more moist consistency.

When *rempah* is well fried, add fried fish pieces and let them steep in *rempah* for a few seconds, stirring gently over low heat. Serve with *rempah* heaped on top of fish.

Baby Shark Curry with Lady's Fingers

Cooking time: 10 minutes

10 lady's fingers
5 tablespoons oil
1 large onion, sliced
2 red chillies | *sliced lengthwise*
2 green chillies | *and seeded*
1 stalk curry leaves
1 thumbsized piece ginger,
    pounded
2 cloves garlic, pounded
half a coconut, grated
200 millilitres water
3 tablespoons tamarind powder
400 millilitres water
500 g shark meat, cut into
    bite-sized chunks
2 teaspoons salt

Rempah
2 tablespoons ground coriander
2 teaspoons ground cummin
2 teaspoons ground aniseed
1 teaspoon chilli powder

Cut stalks off lady's fingers and leave whole.

Heat oil and fry onion, chillies and curry leaves for 1 minute. Add pounded ginger and garlic and *rempah* and fry until fragrant.

Add coconut milk (obtained from squeezing grated coconut with 200 millilitres water) and tamarind powder mixed with 400 millilitres water. Bring to a boil. Add fish, lady's fingers and salt and simmer for 5 minutes.

Whole Pomfret with Sambal

(Illustrated on p. 29)

Cooking time: 15 minutes

1 *bawal hitam* (black pomfret), about
  400 g
4 tablespoons oil
2 tablespoons preserved soy beans
  (Hokkien: *taucheo*), drained and mashed
2 teaspoons sugar
1 tablespoon tamarind powder
300 millilitres water
2 *daun limau purut*, shredded

Rempah
10 dried chillies
5 red chillies
10 shallots
2 cloves garlic
1 stalk lemon grass
1 tablespoon *belacan* powder

Fry whole pomfret in oil for about 8 minutes until brown. Leave aside.

Remove half the oil and fry *rempah* until fragrant. Add preserved soy beans, sugar and tamarind mixed with water. Bring to a boil. Pour *sambal* over pomfret and sprinkle with shredded *daun limau purut*.

Sembilang Masak Pedas

Cooking time: 10 minutes

4 tablespoons oil
2 stalks lemon grass, bruised
3 tablespoons tamarind powder
1 tablespoon tamarind paste
1 litre water
2 whole *sembilang* (catfish)
1 teaspoon salt to remove fish slime
1 teaspoon salt
1 teaspoon sugar
2 turmeric leaves
1 teaspoon black soy sauce

Rempah
5 candlenuts
5 red chillies
15 shallots
5 slices galingale
1 teaspoon ground turmeric
1 tablespoon *belacan* powder

Fry *rempah* in oil until fragrant. Add lemon grass and fry for 1 minute more. Mix both types of tamarind with water and strain liquid. Add liquid to *rempah* and bring to a boil.

While gravy is simmering, gut catfish and cut into large chunks. Rub with salt to remove slime and add to gravy. Simmer for 5 minutes, then add salt, sugar, turmeric leaves and soy sauce. Serve with a dip of *sambal belacan* (p. 86).

Note: Catfish is always sold live and swimming in a tub. Never buy it frozen or iced as the delicate flesh deteriorates very fast. When cleaning it, be extremely careful of the dorsal and pectoral spines as they are needle-sharp and inflict painful wounds.

Sweet-Sour Garoupa

Cooking time: 15 minutes

1 large onion, sliced
2 tomatoes, quartered
1 tablespoon oil
4 pickled leek bulbs
   (Hokkien: *lak keo*), sliced
2 tablespoons canned pineapple
   chunks
1 *garoupa* (grouper), about
   500 g
4 tablespoons cornflour
500 millilitres oil
1 stalk spring onion, cut
   into 4 cm lengths
1 bunch coriander leaves,
   cut into 4 cm lengths

Sauce (mixed)
1 tablespoon plum sauce
   (Hokkien: *boey cheo*)
6 tablespoons pineapple syrup
   (from canned pineapple)
4 tablespoons tomato sauce
1 teaspoon cornflour
350 millilitres water

Fry onion and tomatoes in 1 tablespoon oil. Add sauce and *lak keo* and bring to a boil. Add pineapple and leave aside.

Score deep diagonal cuts on *garoupa*. Dust *garoupa* with cornflour and fry in oil in a clean pan for 10 minutes until crisp and brown.

Place fish in a large, deep dish and pour sauce over after it has been reheated, just before serving. Garnish with spring onion and coriander leaves.

Frying the fish after you have made the sauce leaves you with a dish that is nice and hot. If you fry the fish first you might have to steep it in the sauce while it is boiling in order to serve it hot but you will not get the same crispiness. It is better to pour the sauce over the fish just after it has been fried.

Ikan Masak Asam Pekat

Cooking time: 12 minutes

4 green chillies
3 tablespoons tamarind paste
300 millilitres water
4 *tenggiri* (Spanish mackerel) steaks,
   2 cm thick
1 teaspoon salt
2 teaspoons sugar
1 tomato, quartered
1 tablespoon oil

Rempah
1 large onion
1 teaspoon ground turmeric
1 heaped tablespoon *belacan* powder

Slit chillies lengthwise, seed and remove stalks only. Mix tamarind with water, adding a little more if it is too thick. It should just flow when poured.

Put to a boil and add *rempah*. Simmer for 5 minutes and add chillies and fish (either left whole or cut into chunks) and simmer for 5 minutes. Add salt, sugar and tomatoes in the last 2 minutes of cooking. Add oil last but leave it out if you prefer it clear.

Tenggiri in Hot Bean Paste

Cooking time: 15 minutes

1 whole *tenggiri* (Spanish mackerel),
about 600 g, cut into steaks
5 tablespoons oil
2 tablespoons preserved soy beans
(Hokkien: *taucheo*), washed, drained
and mashed
2 tablespoons sugar
juice of 2 limes
1 cucumber, skinned and sliced

Rempah
6 shallots
2 cloves garlic
4 candlenuts
2 teaspoons *belacan* powder
1 tablespoon chilli powder
1 teaspoon lemon grass powder
1 teaspoon galingale powder

Fry *tenggiri* pieces in oil until cooked.
Assemble pieces on a large dish to form a
whole fish.

In the remaining oil, fry *rempah* until
fragrant and add preserved soy beans. Fry
for another minute. Add sugar and lime
juice and simmer for 2 minutes. Spoon
gravy over fish and garnish with cucumber
slices.

Hot Fish Curry

Cooking time: 12 minutes

1 coconut, grated
300 millilitres water
4 tablespoons oil
1 teaspoon mustard seed
10 shallots
3 cloves garlic } *pounded together*
4 cm piece ginger
½ teaspoon fenugreek
4 tablespoons tamarind powder
200 millilitres water
600 g *kurau* (threadfin)
2 large onions, quartered
2 tomatoes, halved
4 stalks curry leaves
2 brinjals, halved lengthwise

Fish Curry Powder
2 tablespoons chilli powder
5 tablespoons ground coriander
3 tablespoons ground cummin
1 tablespoon ground aniseed
2 teaspoons ground turmeric
1 tablespoon white pepper
4 cardamoms, left whole

Squeeze grated coconut with water for
coconut milk. Set aside.

In hot oil, fry mustard seed over low heat
until they pop. Add pounded shallots, garlic
and ginger, fenugreek, cardamoms and fish
curry powder moistened with a little
coconut milk into a paste. Fry mixture until
fragrant. Add tamarind powder mixed with
water and remaining coconut milk and bring
to a boil.

Add fish, onions, tomatoes, curry leaves
and brinjals during last 5 minutes of
cooking.

OPPOSITE: Udang Goreng Chilli (recipe p. 47).
PAGE 42: Kepeting Bakar (recipe p. 50).

Tamban Goreng Asam

Cooking time: 5 minutes

Tamban is about 10 cm long, dark green above and silvery below with a golden band along each side.

500 g *tamban* **(sprat)**
3 tablespoons tamarind paste
200 millilitres water
1 teaspoon salt (optional)
5 tablespoons oil

Scale and wash fish, removing entrails without taking off the heads. Marinate in tamarind mixed with water and salt (if used) for 20 minutes. Drain but do not wash, and deep-fry for 2 minutes. Serve hot with a squeeze of lime juice on each fish.

Fish Stuffed with Turmeric and Chilli

Cooking time: 10 minutes

1 large *ikan merah* **(red snapper)**
  or *bawal* **(pomfret)**
2 teaspoons salt
4 tablespoons oil

Rempah
4 red chillies
1 small onion
1 teaspoon ground turmeric
1 teaspoon salt

Rub fish with salt to get rid of slime. Wash and slit the stomach to leave a large cavity. Cut deep slits, at a slant, on each side of the body. Stuff all slits and the cavity with *rempah* and fry in hot oil for 4 minutes on each side or until fish's eyes pop out.

Steamed Ikan Bilis with Taucheo and Chilli

Cooking time: 5–10 minutes

200 g ready-steamed *bilis*
  (anchovy)
2 teaspoons preserved soy beans
  (Hokkien: *taucheo***)**
1 teaspoon sugar
juice of 2 limes
2 red chillies, sliced

Re-steam *bilis* for 5 minutes, or if you can find fresh ones, steam them for 10 minutes. Remove head, bone and entrails of each fish and leave aside.

Lightly mash preserved soy beans and add sugar, lime juice and sliced chillies. Pour this mixture over *bilis* and eat with plain porridge.

PAGE 43: Siput Lemak (recipe p. 52).

OPPOSITE: Clockwise from top (on plate), Ikan Panggang with Sambal Kicap (recipe p. 36), Acar (recipe p. 98), Sambal Udang Belimbing (recipe p. 46), Rice and Fried Anchovy. Bottom left, Sambal Belacan (recipe p. 86).

Sambal Udang Belimbing

(Illustrated on p. 44)

Cooking time: 8 minutes

500 g small prawns
½ coconut, grated
400 millilitres water
10 *belimbing buloh* (sour star fruit)
5 tablespoons oil
1 teaspoon salt
1 teaspoon sugar

Ingredients to be Sliced
1 red chilli
1 stalk lemon grass
4 shallots
2 cloves garlic

Rempah
3 red chillies
1 large onion
4 candlenuts
1 tablespoon *belacan* powder

Wash and clean prawns, leaving tails on if you prefer. Squeeze coconut with 400 millilitres water for coconut milk. Cut off tips of each *belimbing buloh* and halve lengthwise, removing the bitter central stalk.

Heat 2 tablespoons of the oil and fry sliced ingredients till brown. Remove to a dish. Fry *rempah* in remaining 3 tablespoons oil until fragrant. Add coconut milk and bring to a boil. Add prawns, *belimbing buloh*, salt and sugar and simmer for 5 minutes. Serve garnished with fried sliced ingredients.

Prawn Compote

Cooking time: 5 minutes

500 g medium-sized prawns
2 tablespoons oil
1 tablespoon preserved soy beans (Hokkien: *taucheo*), washed and mashed lightly
4 tablespoons water
1 teaspoon sugar

Ingredients to be Sliced Fine
1 stalk lemon grass
2 cm piece galingale
3 cm piece stem ginger
2 cm piece turmeric
1 large onion
3 red chillies
2 dried chillies
2 *daun limau purut*
3 cloves garlic

Wash and clean prawns. Remove shell but leave tail on. Fry sliced ingredients in oil for 1 minute. Add prawns, preserved soy beans and water, a little at a time so you will not have too watery a dish. It should have just a hint of gravy. Fry for 2 minutes, then add sugar.

Hot Sambal Goreng

Cooking time: 8 minutes

400 g small prawns
1 teaspoon sugar
3 tablespoons tamarind powder
250 millilitres water
6 belimbing buloh (sour star fruit)
3 tablespoons oil
1 large onion, sliced
1 teaspoon salt
1 tablespoon tomato puree

Rempah
3 large onions
10 dried chillies, soaked in hot water
for 10 minutes
4 red chillies
3 candlenuts
1 tablespoon belacan powder

Wash and devein prawns. Sprinkle sugar on them and leave for 10 minutes. Mix tamarind powder with water. Cut off ends of *belimbing buloh* and halve lengthwise, taking out bitter core.

Fry *rempah* in oil until fragrant. Add sliced onion and fry for one minute. Add tamarind liquid. Bring to a boil. Add prawns, *belimbing buloh*, salt and tomato puree and simmer for 2 minutes.

Salt and Pepper Prawns

Cooking time: 5–8 minutes

500 g medium-sized prawns, washed and
dried thoroughly, with shells on
2 teaspoons good black pepper
2 teaspoons salt
2 tablespoons oil

In a hot pan, dry fry the prawns for 1 minute and cover with a tight lid to cook through. Remove cover and sprinkle with pepper and salt. Stir-fry until prawns are well covered. Add oil and give the pan a good shake so the prawns are well coated with spice and oil. Serve hot.

Udang Goreng Chilli

(Illustrated on p. 41)

Cooking time: 5 minutes

8 large tiger prawns
5 red chillies
3 cloves garlic
1 large onion
3 tablespoons oil
1 teaspoon salt
1 teaspoon sugar

Wash prawns and cut off about 1 cm from the head. Halve each prawn lengthwise. Pound chillies and garlic but not too finely.

Slice onion and fry in oil until soft but not brown. Add the pounded chilli and garlic mixture and lower heat. Fry until fragrant and add prawns, increasing heat at the same time. Stir-fry, sprinkling in a few drops of water if it is too dry. Season, adding sugar last. When the prawns turn light red, they are cooked.

Sambal Grago (Dried Prawn Sambal)

Cooking time: 20 minutes

5 tablespoons oil
400 g dried prawns, soaked in hot water
for 5 minutes and pounded
1 teaspoon sugar
juice of 3 limes

Rempah
5 red chillies
5 dried chillies
2 large onions
2 candlenuts
2 *daun limau purut*
1 tablespoon *belacan* powder

Fry *rempah* in oil for about 2 minutes until fragrant. Add pounded dried prawns and fry for 15 minutes until oil seeps out again. Add sugar and lime juice just before serving with bread. This is an excellent spread for sandwiches.

Prawns Stuffed with Sambal

Cooking time: 4 minutes

500 g medium-sized prawns
10 tablespoons oil

Rempah
5 red chillies
3 *daun limau purut*
1 large onion
4 candlenuts
1 teaspoon ground turmeric
1 tablespoon *belacan* powder

Wash prawns and cut a deep slit down the back, breaking through the shell. Stuff each prawn with *rempah* and deep-fry in oil for 2 minutes until golden brown.

Prawns with Kangkung

Cooking time: 8 minutes

300 g water convolvulus
3 tablespoons oil
300 g small prawns, shelled
400 millilitres water
sugar to taste

Rempah
4 red chillies
2 tablespoons *belacan* powder
1 teaspoon salt

Wash and slice vegetable into 5 cm lengths, making sure to cut through stems. Leeches are known to be fond of hiding in water convolvulus stems.

Fry *rempah* in oil until fragrant and add vegetable. Stir-fry until well coated with oil, then add prawns. Add water and lower heat to simmer for 5 minutes. Add a little sugar if you like a sweet tang to your dish.

Udang Goreng Asam

Cooking time: 1–3 minutes

500 g medium-sized prawns
2 tablespoons tamarind paste (do not use tamarind powder for this dish)
300 millilitres water
½ teaspoon salt
5 tablespoons oil

Clean prawns and cut off whiskers. Mix tamarind with water and salt and marinate prawns in tamarind mixture, covering each prawn well. After half an hour, drain off tamarind. Do not wash or you will have pallid-looking prawns after frying.

Heat oil until smoking and fry prawns for 1–2 minutes until crisp and brown. Drain on absorbent paper.

Crunchy Prawn Curry

Cooking time: 8 minutes

500 g medium-sized prawns
10 *belimbing buloh* (sour star fruit)
150 g French beans, sliced fine diagonally
4 green chillies, left whole
½ coconut, grated
350 millilitres water
1 teaspoon salt

Rempah
2 cloves garlic
2 large onions
1 teaspoon ground turmeric
1 teaspoon galingale powder

Wash and shell prawns. Cut off tips of *belimbing buloh* and halve lengthwise, removing the core. Wash and drain French beans. Remove chilli stalks. Squeeze grated coconut with water for milk.

Put coconut milk to boil for a few minutes, then add *rempah*. When mixture is a little thick (after about 3 minutes), add prawns, beans, chillies and salt. Simmer for 3 minutes or until prawns turn pink.

Udang Lobok Goreng Taucheo

Cooking time: 6 minutes

4 *udang lobok* (slipper or flathead lobster)
2 tablespoons preserved soy beans (Hokkien: *taucheo*)
2 cloves garlic
3 tablespoons oil
1 red chilli, sliced fine
1 teaspoon sugar
300 millilitres water

Wash lobster and, with a sharp knife, cut round the large head and pull off. Use kitchen scissors and cut down the soft, ridged belly. Remove meat in one piece and cut each lobster into 2 or 3 pieces. Wash again and drain.

Crush preserved soy beans and garlic separately. Heat oil and fry garlic till brown, then add preserved soy beans. Add lobster meat and fry for 2 minutes, then add chilli, sugar and water. Simmer for 2 or 3 minutes till lobster turns opaque.

Kepeting Bakar (Baked Crabs)

(Illustrated on p. 42)

Cooking time: 8–15 minutes

**4 crabs (mottled variety,
   Cantonese: *far hai*)**
100 g minced pork
1 stalk spring onion, chopped
1 teaspoon salt
1 teaspoon cornflour
4 tablespoons water
2 tablespoons oil
1 bunch coriander leaves

Steam crabs after washing, and peel off meat and roe. Crack claws with a heavy object and extract all meat. Wash crab shells well and keep.

Mix crabmeat and roe with minced pork, chopped spring onion and salt. Blend cornflour with water and add to mixture.

Stuff crab shells with mixture and brush generously with oil. Grill for 8 minutes or bake in a hot oven for 15 minutes. Alternatively you can deep-fry. This is faster but greasier. Serve with fresh coriander leaves.

Bakwan Kepeting

(Illustrated on p. 18)

Cooking time: 20 minutes

2 large crabs (mottled variety)
150 g prawns
350 g minced pork
2 stalks coriander leaves, chopped fine
1 teaspoon salt
5 tablespoons oil
10 cloves garlic, crushed
1 tablespoon cornflour
3 pieces canned bamboo shoots
2.5 litres water
2 teaspoons salt, or to taste
1 bunch coriander leaves, chopped
black or white pepper

Heat oil and fry garlic until light brown. Scoop out about 2 tablespoonfuls to add to minced meat mixture. Add cornflour and knead well. Stuff crab shells with this mixture. (There should be some left over.)

Wash bamboo shoots and shred very fine. Mix with the leftover stuffing and form into balls the size of walnuts. (If you like, you can mix bamboo shreds with meat paste before stuffing shells.) Leave aside.

Bring water to a boil. (The traditional stock is made with pork bones, but I find this makes the soup over-rich as the flavour from the minced meat, crab and prawn balls is quite enough.)

When water boils, add remaining fried garlic, meatballs and stuffed crab shells. Simmer for 4 minutes and season to taste. Serve with fresh coriander leaves and as much pepper as each diner likes. You may leave the fried garlic last to be added to individual bowls as desired.

Wash crabs and steam for 10 minutes. Remove meat and roe and keep shells. Chop prawns roughly and mix with minced pork, flaked crabmeat, chopped coriander leaves and 1 teaspoon salt.

Crab Fried with Taucheo and Chilli

Cooking time: 10 minutes

3 large crabs, any variety, about 1 kg
4 tablespoons oil
2 tablespoons preserved soy beans
   (Hokkien: *taucheo*),
   washed and mashed
3 red chillies, pounded
450 millilitres water
1 teaspoon sugar

Wash and cut crabs into four pieces. Lightly crack claws but do not break completely. Reserve roe.

Heat oil and fry preserved soy beans and chilli for 2 minutes. Add crab pieces and stir-fry, without adding water, for 2 minutes. When crab turns pink, add water and roe and cover to simmer for 5 minutes. Add sugar last and serve hot.

Sotong Goreng Chilli

Cooking time: 10 minutes

500 g *sotong* (cuttlefish)
3 tablespoons tamarind powder
250 millilitres hot water
3 tablespoons cornflour
5 tablespoons oil
1 teaspoon sugar

Rempah
1 large onion
2 cloves garlic
6 dried chillies
3 candlenuts
2 *daun limau purut*
1 teaspoon lemon grass powder

Wash cuttlefish and remove ink sac. Cut into rings leaving tentacles whole. Marinate in tamarind mixed with hot water for 5 minutes and drain thoroughly. Reserve marinade. Pat dry with kitchen towels and coat liberally with cornflour. Sieve off excess flour and fry in hot oil till crisp. Set aside.

In remaining oil fry *rempah* till fragrant and add reserved marinade a little at a time till gravy is thick. Add sugar. Put fried cuttlefish rings in and simmer for 1 minute.

Kepah Goreng

Cooking time: 3 minutes

The kepah *is a hard-shelled clam known as the Venus shell, and is yellowish brown in colour.*

500 g *kepah* (Venus shell)
3 tablespoons oil
2 cloves garlic, crushed
250 millilitres water
2 teaspoons pepper
1 teaspoon salt

Wash *kepah* well, removing every bit of sand and grit. Heat oil and fry crushed garlic till brown. Add *kepah* and water and stir-fry till all are open. Some may be half-opened but they are still cooked. Add pepper and salt and stir well.

Siput Lemak

(Illustrated on p. 43)

Cooking time: 15 minutes

This delicious member of the mollusc family is probably one of the most maligned seafoods that ever graced a dinner table. Known as siput *in Malay or* koo koo lor *in Teochew, they tend to put off even the most experienced cooks as they are messy to prepare and, when left unattended for a few minutes, have a tendency to crawl all over the kitchen floor and even up walls! Getting at the meat can also be a jaw-aching task as some friends I invited to lunch to try the dish found out. The trick is to make a lusty pucker and, with one mighty breath, suck out the meat. This recipe is of a light coconut gravy called* rempah titiek *which is basically* lemak *with liberal dashes of pepper. Although this is a classic dish there is no reason why you can't substitute with other shellfish of your liking— depending on availability. Try conch or top- shell.*

2 kg *siput* (horn shell or ear shell)
1 coconut, grated
2.5 litres water
6 tablespoons oil
2 stalks lemon grass, bruised
2 teaspoons salt

Rempah
8 red chillies
20 shallots
5 slices galingale or 1 tablespoon
   galingale powder
4 candlenuts
1 tablespoon *belacan* powder
1 tablespoon pepper

Wash *siput* in a large basin. Use a small brush to scrub away the mud they come coated with. It needs several changes of water before you can get them really clean. Using a pair of pliers, cut off ½ cm from the tail end of each *siput*. Drain and leave aside. Squeeze grated coconut with water for coconut milk.

Heat oil in a *kwali* and fry *rempah* until fragrant. Add lemon grass and *siput* and fry for 2 minutes. Add coconut milk and bring to a boil. Simmer for 10 minutes and add salt. A simple way to eat *siput* is to use small sharp-tined forks to dig out the meat.

Pork, Beef and Mutton

That Straits cuisine is borrowed a great deal from Malay cuisine is undeniable but it needed the best of ingenuity on the part of the Nonyas to adapt the many spice blends to a favourite meat of the Chinese—pork. Perhaps the most fragrant example of this marriage of cuisines is Satay Babi or Pork Satay.

Not content to have merely beef, chicken or mutton satay which they learnt to make from eating of much Malay satay using these three meats, the Nonya of my era set out to create what is today a classic. And since sit-down meals were the *raison d'être* for gatherings of the Nonya clan, my mother and aunts fried up the most delicious satay. Tourists might have been initiated into this exotic food of our country with skewered satay but few can have tasted Satay Babi Goreng. Around this was built such complements as cucumber salads, tamarind marinated deep-fried fish and always rice.

Friends from abroad today ask me how the Nonya ladies stayed slim (the portly ones were usually grandmothers) when they ate so much fatty pork. I cannot resist the tongue-in-cheek reply that Straitsborn pork said 'sarong' to its fat a long time ago! Seriously, the pork dishes I used to eat at our home had most of the fat trimmed off and just enough left to make the dish moist without being greasy. Besides, the spices soaked up what excess fat there was, leaving a thickish *rempah* that made delicious spreads on bread.

When we did eat pork with all its fat, it was invariably in a dish that had a balance of sour things. A classic example is Itek Tim which is a duck soup with salted Tientsin vegetable into which were thrown a leg of pork and several pieces of belly cuts. It would seem like so much grease, but the *kiam chye* (salted vegetable) tempered this greasiness remarkably. It would also have one or two preserved sour limes that further heightened the oily soup, and when drunk with fresh green chilli (some imbibed with a dash of good brandy in a bowl of soup), it has to be the best tasting of soups.

Far from being a revolting discard, pig's skin was rendered into a delicacy that belies any western description of 'eating chopped up handbag'. He has not lived who has not eaten pork skin (pig's skin is not an apt description at all) with cucumber and *sambal belacan*. I fear this interesting and ingenious salad is going down the troughs for all the care modern Singaporeans accord pork skin. I never tell my pork man to skin any pork I buy and he, the well-meaning man, invariably has to be stopped cutting that good flap of pink epidermis away.

As for offal, far from regarding liver as an unctuous remedy for anaemia, Straitsborn cuisine has elevated the art of cooking such meats to great heights. Lungs with shredded bamboo shoots, liver with coriander in caul lining, steamed and deep-fried, kidney in soup redolent with ginger—these are great dishes that took pride of place on festive occasions. How well I remember my mother (bless her culinary skills which I shall miss dearly) taking great pains to clean a pair of kidneys till the ammonia smell was but a faint tang. Sliced and artfully cooked in soup that had just a few slices of good liver and plenty of ginger, it made a hearty late night snack or birthday breakfast dish.

Even pig's ears, once cleaned of gristle and hair, went into a soy sauce that stewed the chewy appendages into tasty titbits that were dipped in a special chilli and garlic sauce. When my family had hard times, the pork man would give my mother a large ear for nothing and this would be our entire meal with, of course, plain congee. I still eat this dish, not to cock a snook at middle-

class pretension, but because I genuinely enjoy the delightful contrast of taste and flavours. The stew had galingale root boiled in a gravy that was first sugar caramelized until brown, then had good soy sauce added.

But it is to spices I turn to today when faced with a hunk of pork of this cut or that. What remains my favourite is Pork à la Shiok—for want of a better name—on page 67 which has the seven basic ingredients and spices of onion, garlic, galingale, chilli, *belacan*, candlenuts and lemon grass. With bottled spices, I enjoy this more often than before.

Babi Hong

Cooking time: 40 minutes

3 cloves garlic, crushed
1 large onion, sliced fine
2 tablespoons oil
2 tablespoons preserved soy beans
  (Hokkien: *taucheo*), washed and
  pounded
500 g foreleg of pork (Hokkien: *tui bak*)
1 teaspoon sugar
1 teaspoon five-spice powder
1 litre water
3 green chillies

Brown garlic and onion in hot oil and add preserved soy beans. Add pork, fry for a few minutes then add remaining ingredients except chillies. Simmer for 35 minutes and serve with green chillies broken into pieces.

Pork, Cucumber and Egg Drop Soup

Cooking time: 15 minutes

200 g lean pork
1 cucumber
800 millilitres water
2 eggs
1 teaspoon salt or 1 teaspoon fish sauce
1 teaspoon pepper
½ chicken bouillon cube
1 teaspoon salted winter vegetable
  (Hokkien: *tang chye*)

Cut pork into bite-sized pieces. Skin cucumber, remove soft centre and slice into bite-sized pieces. Bring water to a boil and add pork. After pork has simmered for 10 minutes, add cucumber. Beat each egg separately and pour into the simmering soup in a stream. Add all other ingredients and serve garnished with *tang chye*.

Deep-fried Meatballs in Pig's Caul

(Illustrated on p. 61)

Cooking time: 8–10 minutes

2 sheets pig's caul (Cantonese: *chee mong yeow*)
400 g minced pork
250 g prawns, minced
10 water chestnuts, minced
1 teaspoon salt
1 teaspoon monosodium glutamate
1 tablespoon cornflour ⎫ *mixed*
100 millilitres water ⎬
2 eggs, beaten
500 g fine breadcrumbs
oil for deep-frying

You may have to order pig's caul from the butcher a day in advance as it is a popular item, especially among the Cantonese. Soak in plenty of water and remove all foreign matter. Drain and spread out on a flat surface.

Mix minced pork, prawns and water chestnuts thoroughly. Add seasoning and cornflour mixture and taste after boiling a small amount in water. Adjust seasoning.

Spread 2 tablespoons of the mixture on caul and make up into rolls, each about 18 cm long. You should get about 6 rolls. Steam for 5 minutes.

Allow to cool and cut each roll into four 4 cm pieces. Dip each piece in egg and roll in breadcrumbs. Repeat once to get a second coating. Heat oil till smoking and deep-fry until light brown. Remove with a slotted spoon and serve with a dip of half oyster and half tomato sauce.

Hati Babi Bungkus

(Illustrated on pp. 19, 61)

Cooking time: 6 minutes

10 shallots, pounded till fine
4 tablespoons oil for frying shallots
200 g minced pork
300 g pig's liver, boiled and diced very fine
1 teaspoon salt
1 teaspoon sugar
1 tablespoon black soy sauce
1 teaspoon vinegar
2 tablespoons ground coriander, dry-fried till fragrant
2 teaspoons pepper
1 sheet pig's caul
oil for deep-frying

Fry pounded shallots in oil till light brown but not crisp. Mix with minced pork, liver, salt, sugar, soy sauce, vinegar, coriander and pepper.

Wash and clean pig's caul, removing all dirt and gristle. Pat dry and spread over flat surface. Using caul, wrap mixture into individual balls the size of walnuts, making sure each is well sealed.

Heat oil and deep-fry balls for 3 minutes on each side. Serve with *sambal kuakchye* (p. 99).

Soybean Cakes Stuffed with Spicy Minced Pork

Cooking time: 16 minutes

4 pieces firm soybean cakes
  (Hokkien: *taukwa*)
200 g minced pork
1 teaspoon salt
1 egg
5 tablespoons oil
½ cucumber, sliced

Rempah
10 shallots
4 candlenuts
1 teaspoon *belacan* powder
1 teaspoon chilli powder
1 teaspoon ground aniseed
1 teaspoon ground cummin
2 tablespoons ground coriander

Cut each soybean cake square into 2 triangles. Slit down the broadest side of each triangle and scoop out a little of the cake to make a pocket.

Mix minced pork with *rempah* and salt. Break egg into a separate container and beat lightly. Add beaten egg to pork mixture to bind.

Stuff each soybean cake triangle with pork mixture and steam for 10 minutes. Cool and fry in hot oil until light brown. Serve with cucumber slices and a dip of chilli sauce.

Lemak Bittergourd Stuffed with Minced Pork

Cooking time: 10 minutes

1 piece lard, about 4 × 4 × 1 cm
150 g minced pork
100 g shrimps, shelled and minced
2 teaspoons cornflour
1 teaspoon salt
1 bittergourd
water for scalding
½ coconut, grated
800 millilitres water
3 tablespoons oil

Rempah
1 large onion
4 candlenuts
1 teaspoon chilli powder
½ teaspoon ground turmeric

Chop lard and mix with minced pork, shrimps, cornflour and salt.

Cut bittergourd into circles 2 cm thick and remove pith and seeds. Boil a little water and scald pieces by dipping once. Stuff each piece with minced pork mixture and leave aside. Squeeze coconut with water for coconut milk.

Heat *kwali* with oil and fry *rempah* until fragrant. Add coconut milk and bring to a boil. Add bittergourd pieces and simmer for 5 minutes. Do not overcook or the pork will become hard.

Tauyu Bak with Tau Pok
(Stewed Pork with Dried Soybean Cakes)

(Illustrated on p. 62)

Cooking time: 40 minutes

For this recipe, use a heavy-bottomed deep pot if you have one so you don't have to transfer pork after cooking in a kwali. The meat is usually cut into large chunks, but size is really a matter of taste. Personally, I prefer the pork in pieces I don't need to cut again after cooking. Another point worth remembering when cooking any kind of soy sauce pork is that the meat should be well coated with soy sauce before water is added. Insufficient sauteeing will result in pale-looking pork instead of succulent chunks.

2 tablespoons oil
4 cloves garlic, bruised slightly
500 g foreleg of pork (Hokkien: *tui bak*),
    cut into chunks
4 tablespoons black soy sauce
1.5 litres water
6 pieces dried soybean cakes (Hokkien:
    tau pok)
salt to taste
hardboiled eggs (optional)

Heat oil. Lightly brown garlic, then add pork. When pork has been well sealed by hot oil, add soy sauce and stew for 5 minutes, stirring to prevent burning. Pork should be well coated with sauce.

If you have been using a *kwali* for the first step, transfer meat to a deep pot. Add water and leave to simmer for 45 minutes. In the last 10 minutes of cooking, add dried soybean cakes, either whole or cut into triangles. Continue to simmer over low heat until soup reaches the consistency desired. It may be necessary to add salt if the soy sauce you use is not salty enough. Taste as you season.

Additional ingredients like hardboiled eggs stretch the dish to feed more people. You can add these the next day when reheating.

Fried Pork with Liver and Onions

Cooking time: 4 minutes

250 g lean pork
100 g liver
1 tablespoon soy sauce
1 large onion, sliced
4 slices ginger, cut into strips
2 tablespoons oil
200 millilitres water
1 teaspoon fish sauce
1 stalk spring onion
1 teaspoon cornflour
1 tablespoon water

Slice pork and liver into thin pieces and marinate in soy sauce.

Fry onion with ginger in oil. Add pork and liver and fry on high heat until liver changes colour. It should take about 1 minute. Add water, fish sauce and spring onion cut into 3 cm lengths. Mix cornflour with a little water and add to pan, letting the gravy thicken. Serve hot.

Spiced Roast Pork

Cooking time: 35 minutes

800 g pork with skin, preferably belly pork
2 teaspoons vinegar
1 teaspoon salt
1 teaspoon black pepper
1 tablespoon ground coriander
1 teaspoon ground cinnamon
2 cloves garlic, pounded fine
1 tablespoon honey
1 tablespoon black soy sauce
1 teaspoon light soy sauce
2 tablespoons oil
water for roasting pan

Slightly chill pork and score across back of skin ½ cm deep. Rub vinegar, salt and pepper on skin. Mix all other ingredients except water and rub all over pork.

Pre-heat oven to Gas Mark 4. Put water in roasting pan and roast pork on a wire rack over the pan. Roast for 20 minutes, then lower heat for 15 minutes to finish cooking. Test with skewer. Meat should not be pink.

Babi Pong Teh
(Pork with Taucheo)

(Illustrated on p. 62)

Cooking time: 40 minutes

700 g foreleg of pork (Hokkien: *tui bak*),
** with skin**
2 pieces sugar-cane, each 8 cm
3 tablespoons oil
10 shallots, sliced fine
4 cloves garlic, pounded
1 tablespoon preserved soy beans
** (Hokkien: *taucheo*), washed,**
** drained and pounded**
1 teaspoon ground cinnamon
2 tablespoons black soy sauce
1.5 litres water
1 teaspoon salt
1 teaspoon sugar
1 can bamboo shoots (optional)
green chillies

Cut pork into large chunks with skin left on. Skin and wash sugar-cane.

Heat oil in a *kwali* and fry shallots until light brown but not crispy. Add garlic and preserved soy beans and fry for 2 minutes until mixture is fragrant. Add pork and ground cinnamon and fry for a few more minutes. Add soy sauce and water and simmer for 10 minutes. Add sugar-cane, salt and sugar and leave to simmer until pork is tender. (If you cannot find sugar-cane, substitute with a piece of rock sugar the size of a walnut.)

Add bamboo shoots cut into chunks to stretch the dish. The classic way to serve this dish is with green chillies broken (not cut) into pieces. It is eaten with French bread.

Pork Tempera

Cooking time: 15 minutes

3 tablespoons oil
2 red chillies ⎫
2 cloves garlic ⎬ *sliced*
1 large onion ⎪ *fine*
4 slices ginger ⎭
1 teaspoon *belacan* powder
1 stalk lemon grass, bruised
1 tablespoon black soy sauce
1 teaspoon light soy sauce
juice of 3 limes ⎫ *mixed*
275 millilitres water ⎭
500 g lean pork, fillet or chop, sliced thin
2 teaspoons sugar

Heat oil and fry sliced items, adding *belacan*, lemon grass and soy sauces after 5 minutes. Lastly, add lime water, pork and sugar to simmer for 10 minutes.

If you want a drier, crispier pork, fry meat in a little oil first until surfaces are well sealed.

Pork with Pineapple and Green Chillies

Cooking time: 8 minutes

300 g belly pork
4 green chillies
2 pieces pineapple
1 tablespoon oil
1 clove garlic, crushed
1 tablespoon cornflour
200 millilitres water
1 teaspoon salt
½ teaspoon monosodium glutamate

Cut belly pork into bite-sized pieces. Slice green chillies lengthwise and discard pith containing seeds. Cut pineapple into 1 cm thick wedges.

Heat oil in a *kwali* and fry garlic when it begins to smoke. Put in pork and fry for 3 minutes until it changes colour. Add pineapple pieces and fry for another minute, then add green chillies. Mix cornflour with a little water. Add the rest of the water to pork and pineapple. Simmer, then add cornflour mixture. When sauce has thickened, add salt and monosodium glutamate. Serve hot.

Note: Chicken liver cooked this way is very tasty. Other ingredients you can use are prawns, chicken gizzards and all types of liver. Deboned chicken also makes a nice change.

Lor Bak
(Stewed Pork)

Cooking time: 1 hour
20 minutes in pressure cooker

2 tablespoons sugar
1 kg belly pork
3 tablespoons black soy sauce
1 piece galingale, the size of a walnut
2 slices ginger
1 teaspoon salt
1.5 litres water

Heat *kwali* until very hot and put in sugar to caramelize. Stir vigorously with a wooden spoon to prevent it from burning too fast. Lower heat if it turns dark too quickly.

Put whole piece of pork in to sear. If it is too large, cut it into two long pieces. When pork is well coated with caramel, add soy sauce a little at a time so pork is slowly steeped in it. Add galingale (either whole and bruised or in slices), ginger and salt. When mixture is fragrant with a slight bitter tang, add water and leave to simmer over low heat.

If you have a pressure cooker, add half the amount of liquid specified and cook under pressure so you save more than half the time. Normal simmering takes about 1 hour but with the pressure cooker your pork will be ready in 20 minutes.

Fried Pepper Pork

Cooking time: 8 minutes

500 g lean pork
2 cm piece ginger
2 tablespoons oil
1 clove garlic, crushed
1 tablespoon black pepper
2 teaspoons sugar
1 teaspoon black soy sauce

Cut pork into chunks or slices. If you can get a strip of pork fat from the butcher, slice this and add in for a more moist dish. Cut ginger into fine strips.

Heat oil and fry garlic and ginger until light brown. Add pork pieces and lower heat to fry for a few more minutes. Add pepper, sugar and soy sauce and continue frying over low heat until almost dry.

The meat can be kept in an airtight bottle and eaten as a relish or as a sandwich filling.

OPPOSITE: Left to right, Hati Babi Bungkus (recipe p. 55) and Deep-fried Meatballs in Pig's Caul (recipe p. 55).

PAGE 62: Left to right, Tauyu Bak with Tau Pok (recipe p. 57) and Babi Pong Teh (recipe p. 58).

Opor Babi

Cooking time: 40 minutes

1 kg leg of pork
1 coconut, grated
500 millilitres water
6 *belimbing buloh* (sour star fruit)
1 stalk lemon grass, bruised
1 bay leaf
2 teaspoons salt
2 tablespoons tamarind powder
200 millilitres water

Rempah
3 red chillies (optional)
10 candlenuts
2 medium-sized onions
4 cloves garlic
2 tablespoons ground coriander
1 teaspoon ground fennel
2 teaspoons galingale powder
1 tablespoon *belacan* powder

Cut pork into chunks or thick slices, depending on presentation desired. Squeeze coconut with water for milk.

Blend *rempah* with coconut milk and bring to a boil. Add pork and simmer for 30 minutes. Add *belimbing buloh*, either whole or halved lengthwise (with bitter central pith removed), bruised lemon grass, bay leaf and salt. You can add tamarind mixed with water either together with coconut milk or at any time after that.

There is a variation which requires frying of the spices before adding coconut milk and tamarind liquid. A fine touch comes from using 4 tablespoons grated coconut (without brown skin). Gently fry this in a dry pan until golden brown. Pound it until fine. After the Opor is cooked, sprinkle this on top just before serving.

Babi Chin

Cooking time: 80 minutes
*   30 minutes in pressure cooker*

5 tablespoons oil
3 large onions, pounded coarsely
6 cloves garlic, crushed
1 tablespoon ground coriander mixed with
   water into a paste
1 tablespoon preserved soy beans
   (Hokkien: *taucheo*), washed and
   mashed
2 pig's fore-trotters, cut into 5 cm pieces
2 tablespoons black soy sauce
1 tablespoon sugar
2 litres water
1 teaspoon salt (use if required)

Heat oil. Fry onions and garlic until brown then add coriander and preserved soy beans. Stir-fry for 2 minutes and add trotters. Fry until all pieces are well coated and brown. Add soy sauce, sugar and water.

Simmer for 1½ hours until trotters are tender. Taste for seasoning and if not salty enough, add 1 teaspoon salt or to taste. Some types of preserved soy beans are very salty so do not add salt until after last minute tasting. To cut down cooking time, use a pressure cooker but reduce liquid by one-third.

PAGE 63: Rebong Lemak with Pork Ribs (recipe p. 68).
Bottom left, Teehee Char Rebong (recipe p. 69).

OPPOSITE: Fried Minced Beef with Kiam Chye and Tomato (recipe p. 71).

Lemon Pork

Cooking time: 10 minutes

500 g lean pork with some fat
1 lemon
3 tablespoons palm sugar
1 thumbsized piece ginger, crushed
1 teaspoon salt
1 teaspoon pepper
1 tablespoon Chinese wine or sherry

Cut pork into medium-sized slices. Squeeze juice from lemon and cut a few wedges of lemon rind. Mix lemon juice and rind with all the other ingredients except pork. Marinate pork slices in this mixture. Drain through a colander after 1 hour. Reserve marinade.

Lay pork slices on grill pan and grill for 10 minutes, turning once after 5 minutes. Use marinade to baste occasionally. Serve with cucumber slices or as a sandwich filling.

Fried Asam Pork

Cooking time: 15 minutes

500 g foreleg of pork (Hokkien: *tui bak*)
1 large onion
2 cloves garlic
1 cm piece ginger
2 tablespoons black soy sauce
2 tablespoons tamarind powder
200 millilitres water
½ teaspoon salt
2 tablespoons palm sugar
4 tablespoons oil

Slice pork thinly. Chop onion, garlic and ginger. Blend with soy sauce, tamarind powder, water, salt and sugar.

Heat oil in a *kwali* and fry pork until almost cooked. It should still have a pink tinge to it. Add the blended ingredients. Simmer until almost dry. If you like a less oily dish, drain off oil after frying pork.

Sambal Goreng Babi

Cooking time: 15 minutes

500 g fillet or lean pork
3 tablespoons tamarind powder
250 millilitres water
3 tablespoons oil
1 teaspoon sugar
1 teaspoon salt
4 slices pineapple

Rempah
3 large onions
15 dried chillies
4 candlenuts

Slice pork into 1 cm thick pieces. Mix tamarind powder with water. Heat oil in *kwali* and fry *rempah* until fragrant. Add pork and fry for a few minutes more. Add tamarind liquid a little at a time and until the consistency desired is reached. Add sugar and salt and serve with pineapple slices.

Pork à la Shiok

Cooking time: 40 minutes

Neither my grandmother nor my mother had a name for this delicious dish which has been my mainstay for years. It is one of the few dry curries that can be kept for weeks in the refrigerator and reheated each time to taste even better than before. Perhaps it's the combination of spices or the long frying process, but there's nothing quite like it in any other cuisine. One thing I have learnt from this recipe is to make a lot of it when the mood strikes me.

2 kg belly pork, skinned
5 tablespoons oil
1 teaspoon salt
1 tablespoon sugar

Rempah
6 cloves garlic
3 large onions
10 candlenuts
20 dried chillies
2 tablespoons *belacan* powder
2 tablespoons galingale powder
1 tablespoon lemon grass powder

Chill the belly pork after it has been skinned and washed. This makes it easier to cut even slices, about 1 cm thick, across the grain to get a good balance of lean and fat pork.

Heat a *kwali* and put in pork to fry quickly for about 5 minutes. This is to let the moisture in the pork evaporate and semi-cook it—an important step. Meanwhile blend all spices until fine. Remove pork from *kwali*.

Heat oil until smoking and put in *rempah* to fry over low heat. Fry for 10 minutes until oil seeps out again and add the pork. Now comes the hard part. You need a strong right arm to fry the mixture for a good 30 minutes until it is a rich, red colour. Add salt and sugar towards the end of frying.

It is delicious eaten with bread or rice. Keep the spiced pork in an enamel bowl and refrigerate. Simply reheat a little at a time when you serve it again.

Note: You may increase or decrease the amount of spices and sugar to taste. Some people like it redolent with spices and others prefer just a little.

Dry Pork Curry

Cooking time: 35 minutes

300 g pork chop, without bone
2 teaspoons sugar
2 potatoes
1 carrot
¼ coconut, grated
300 millilitres water
5 shallots
2 cm piece ginger
4 tablespoons oil
2 tablespoons meat curry powder (p. 15)
2 tablespoons water
1 teaspoon salt

Slice pork thinly and marinate in a little sugar. Peel and quarter potatoes and slice carrots into 3 cm chunks. Squeeze coconut with water for milk. Finely shred shallots and ginger.

Fry ginger and shallots in oil until light brown and add curry powder moistened with a little water. Fry until fragrant and add coconut milk. Bring to a boil and add all other ingredients. Simmer for 30 minutes.

Pork Curry

Cooking time: 35 minutes

500 g pork chops, without bone
2 large potatoes
1 coconut, grated
1.5 litres water
4 tablespoons oil
3 cm piece stem ginger, shredded fine
1 large onion, sliced fine
1 teaspoon salt
3 *daun limau purut*

Rempah
2 tablespoons chilli powder
2 tablespoons ground coriander
1 tablespoon ground aniseed
1 tablespoon ground cummin

Cut pork into 2 cm thick slices. Peel and quarter potatoes and dry well. Squeeze coconut with water for coconut milk.

Fry potatoes in oil until slightly brown. Remove and fry ginger and onion until almost brown. Remove.

Blend *rempah* with a little coconut milk and fry in remaining oil until oil seeps out again. Add pork and fry for a few more minutes. Add remaining coconut milk, salt, *daun limau purut*, potatoes, ginger and onion. Simmer for 25 minutes.

Note: The amount of liquid in *lemak* curries is not the important part as some people like a watery curry for mixing with rice and others prefer a thickish, almost dry consistency.

Rebong Lemak with Pork Ribs

(Illustrated on p. 63)

Cooking time: 40 minutes

3 pieces canned bamboo shoot
500 g pork ribs
300 g small prawns
1 coconut, grated
1.5 litres water
4 tablespoons oil
2 teaspoons salt
1 teaspoon sugar

Rempah
15 dried chillies
5 red chillies
2 teaspoons lemon grass powder
1 teaspoon galingale powder
2 teaspoons *belacan* powder
2 teaspoons pepper
1 teaspoon ground turmeric
2 tablespoons ground coriander

Slice bamboo shoots into ½ cm thick pieces and wash and drain. Trim off excess fat from pork ribs and shell prawns. Squeeze coconut with water for approximately 2 litres coconut milk.

Heat oil and fry *rempah* until fragrant. Add pork ribs and fry for a few minutes more until they are thoroughly coated with *rempah*. Add coconut milk and simmer for 35 minutes. Add bamboo shoot midway so they won't get too soft. Add salt and sugar last.

Satay Babi Goreng

(Illustrated on p. 19)

Cooking time: 30 minutes

700 g lean pork, with a little fat
1 coconut, grated
400 millilitres water
2 *daun limau purut*
100 millilitres water (use if required)

Rempah
4 stalks lemon grass or 1 tablespoon
   lemon grass powder
4 red chillies
10 dried chillies
4 candlenuts
15 shallots
2 teaspoons *belacan* powder
2 teaspoons ground aniseed
1 teaspoon ground cummin
2 tablespoons ground coriander
1 teaspoon salt
½ teaspoon pepper
2 teaspoons sugar

Slice pork into 1 cm thick pieces, making sure there is some fat on each piece. Marinate pork in spices for 10 minutes. Meanwhile, squeeze coconut with water for milk but do not discard shreds yet.

Put coconut milk in a heavy-bottomed pot and add the marinated pork and *daun limau purut*. Bring to a boil and lower heat to simmer for 20 minutes. If you use a non-stick pot you need not stir frequently.

If the mixture seems too dry, squeeze a little more milk from the reserved coconut shreds with perhaps 100 millilitres water. Add to the pot and adjust seasoning to taste. When cooked, Satay Babi should be dry but with a gravy that is thick and redolent with fragrant oil.

Teehee Char Rebong
(Pig's Lungs Fried with Bamboo Shoots)

(Illustrated on p. 63)

Cooking time: 15 minutes

1 pair pig's lungs
4 tablespoons oil
5 cloves garlic, crushed
1 piece ginger, about 3 × 2 cm, shredded
2 tablespoons preserved soy beans
   (Hokkien: *taucheo*), washed and
   mashed lightly
200 g streaky pork, boiled and cut into
   slices or strips
200 g canned bamboo shoots, cut into
   strips
150 g prawns, shelled and deveined
1 teaspoon sugar
1 teaspoon fish sauce
½ teaspoon salt
250 millilitres water

Boil lungs in a large pot of water, skimming froth from pot every few minutes. It should take about 5 minutes. Remove and leave to cool. Wash under tap and drain. Cut into thin strips, removing white gristle.

Heat oil and fry garlic and ginger until fragrant. Add preserved soy beans and fry for 1 minute. Add pork, bamboo shoots, prawns and lungs. Stir-fry for 3 minutes and add remaining ingredients. Simmer for 5 minutes until liquid is reduced.

Pork Ribs with Buah Keluak

(Illustrated on p. 19)

Cooking time: ¾ – 1 hour

20 *buah keluak*
3 litres water
6 tablespoons tamarind paste
1 litre water
4 tablespoons oil
1 kg pork ribs
2 teaspoons salt
2 lumps rock sugar, about the size of walnuts

Rempah
6 candlenuts
5 large onions
20 dried chillies or 1 heaped tablespoon chilli powder
2 tablespoons galingale powder
1 teaspoon ground turmeric
1 tablespoon *belacan* powder
1 tablespoon lemon grass powder

Buah keluak should be scrubbed absolutely clean and preferably soaked overnight in 3 litres water but about 5 or 6 hours will do if you don't have time. Scrub clean and, using a sharp instrument, cut away the nut mouth. Leave prepared nuts in the same water for half an hour, and drain but don't throw away water, as it can be used for gravy. Squeeze tamarind with 1 litre water.

Heat oil in a *kwali* and fry *rempah* over low heat until fragrant. Add nuts to fry for a few minutes and then the pork ribs. When meat is well-coated with the spices, add tamarind water, water used to soak *buah keluak*, and salt. Simmer for 1 hour and add rock sugar, a little at a time.

For *buah keluak* to be at its best, serve the next day, after it has been left to simmer slowly.

Beef Rendang

Cooking time: ¾ – 1 hour

1 kg sirloin or rump steak
1½ coconuts, grated
1.5 litres water
2 stalks lemon grass, bruised
4 *daun limau purut*
3 slices galingale
1 teaspoon salt
1 teaspoon sugar

Rempah
15 dried chillies
2 large onions
2 cloves garlic
3 cm piece ginger
2 teaspoons ground coriander
½ teaspoon ground turmeric

Cut beef into 4 cm cubes. Squeeze coconut with water for milk. Put all ingredients into a non-stick pot and simmer, uncovered, until gravy reaches a thick consistency. It should take about 1 hour if you use sirloin. Tougher cuts of beef take a little longer and the dish also becomes more oily as the coconut milk is boiled down.

Fried Minced Beef with Kiam Chye and Tomato

(Illustrated on p. 64)

Cooking time: 5 minutes

200 g minced beef
1 tablespoon cornflour ⎱ *mixed*
3 tablespoons water ⎰
100 g salted vegetable (Hokkien:
  kiam chye)
2 tablespoons oil
2 cloves garlic, crushed
1 tomato, cut into wedges
1 red chilli, sliced
1 teaspoon fish sauce
200 millilitres water

Mix minced beef with cornflour paste. Cut *kiam chye* into strips and soak in water for 5 minutes.

Heat oil and fry crushed garlic until brown. Squeeze *kiam chye* dry and add to this to fry for 2 minutes. Add tomato and beef mixture and stir-fry for 1 minute. Add chilli and seasoning and stir once more before adding water to simmer for 2 minutes.

Hot Beef Curry

Cooking time: 30 minutes

600 g stewing beef, cut into thin slices
1 tablespoon meat curry paste (p. 15)
1 coconut, grated
900 millilitres water
8 tablespoons oil
3 medium-sized potatoes, skinned and
  quartered
3 slices ginger, grated
1 onion, grated
7 tablespoons meat curry paste (p. 15)
2 teaspoons salt

Using the blunt edge of a heavy knife, tenderise beef a little. Mix well with 1 tablespoon curry paste. Set aside. Squeeze coconut with water for milk.

Heat oil and fry potatoes till they turn brown but are still not fully cooked. Remove.

In remaining oil, fry ginger and onion till light brown. Add curry paste and fry till fragrant. Add coconut milk and bring to a boil. Add beef and salt and simmer for about 20 minutes. (The time depends on the cut of beef.) Add half-cooked potatoes in the last 10 minutes of cooking.

Beef Satay

Cooking time: 8–10 minutes

1 kg beef (sirloin or rump)
20 *satay* **skewers**
1 stalk lemon grass, bruised
oil for basting

Rempah
2 cloves garlic
1 large onion
3 candlenuts
2 teaspoons ground cummin
2 teaspoons ground aniseed
2 tablespoons ground coriander
1 tablespoon sugar
1 teaspoon salt

Slice beef into thin pieces about 3 × 2 cm. Marinate in *rempah* for 1 hour, turning occasionally. Using *satay* skewers (*lidi* sticks), thread five or six pieces of beef on each. You should get about 20 skewers of *satay*.

Heat grill and barbecue skewers of beef for about 5 minutes each side. Bruise a stalk of lemon grass and dip in oil to baste as you grill.

Serve Beef Satay with Satay Gravy (this page) and sliced cucumbers.

Satay Gravy

Cooking time: 10 minutes

¼ coconut, grated
250 millilitres water
2 tablespoons oil
4 tablespoons tamarind powder
800 millilitres water
1 teaspoon salt
6 pieces peanut brittle or 4 tablespoons chunky peanut butter mixed with 1 tablespoon sugar

Rempah
15 dried chillies
3 cloves garlic
2 large onions
2 teaspoons galingale powder
1 tablespoon *belacan* **powder**

Squeeze coconut with 250 millilitres water for coconut milk. Fry *rempah* in oil until fragrant. Mix tamarind with water and add to *rempah*. Add coconut milk and salt and simmer for 5 minutes. Pound peanut brittle until fine and add to liquid. If you cannot be bothered to pound peanut brittle, use an equal amount of chunky peanut butter but add 1 tablespoon sugar.

Mutton Rendang

Cooking time: 45 minutes

New Zealand lamb can be used for this dish if you find the smell of mutton too strong for your taste.

1 kg mutton or lamb
1 coconut, grated
2 litres water
2 limes
4 daun limau purut
3 teaspoons sugar
2 teaspoons salt

Rempah

20 dried chillies
5 red chillies
8 slices ginger
2 stalks lemon grass
4 large onions
4 cloves garlic
2 teaspoons ground turmeric
2 teaspoons galingale powder

Cut meat into fairly large pieces (they shrink during slow cooking).

Squeeze coconut with 500 millilitres of the water for first milk. (In slow stewing or cooking, you add thick milk last so the dish does not become too oily.) Add the rest of the water and squeeze out thin milk. Squeeze lime juice into thick milk and allow to curdle a little.

Put meat in with thin milk, *rempah* and *daun limau purut* to simmer. Use a non-stick deep pot so you don't have to keep stirring so often. When liquid has reduced by about half, add thick milk and simmer for another 15 minutes. Add sugar and salt and simmer till gravy is really thick.

Poultry

Much as I miss the days when my family always had a clutch of chickens, a few ducks, and even the occasional piglet rooting in our backyard, I am thankful for the fact that chickens are so easy and cheap to buy today. Whether they are range-reared or battery force-fed is something few of us can control. Generally, supermarket chickens are flavourful with the exception of the odd few that turn out to be *kayu* (wooden) and tasteless. Whatever the variety, in Nonya cooking, with all its wondrous blends of herbs and spices, even the most *kayu* chicken turns out quite decent, if not magnificent.

Ducks, however, are a different story, not having as many *aficionados* as its pecking cousin, having a rather strong smell. Few people are inclined to buy duck as it takes a long time to cook, but few dishes can beat the Nonya Itek Sio (stewed duck in coriander) or Itek Tim (duck soup with salted vegetable). Other than these two dishes, the duck does not make a frequent appearance on a Nonya table, generally lending itself to a wider range of dishes in the hands of Cantonese and Teochew cooks. The famous Pipa Duck and Peking duck are difficult to prepare unless you have those enormous clay ovens required to slowly roast them to perfection. I have, however, learnt from my Cantonese mother-in-law how to stew a duck with mushrooms and chestnuts. While this is a classic dish, there is no reason why you should not substitute chicken instead and come up with perhaps a dish even better than if you had used a duck. There is still less reason why you cannot use pre-packed chicken wings and frying joints to cook the dozen-and-one Nonya curries that call for whole chicken.

Deep-fried Chicken

Cooking time: 8–10 minutes

1 chicken, about 1 kg
2 tablespoons black soy sauce
1 tablespoon Chinese wine (Cantonese: *fa chiew*) or sherry
3 cm piece ginger, pounded for juice
1 teaspoon salt
oil for deep-frying

Wash and clean chicken. Marinate in soy sauce, wine, ginger juice and salt for 1 hour. Drain and hang to dry for half an hour. Deep-fry in smoking hot oil for 2 minutes, then reduce heat to cook inside for another 6 minutes. Chicken should be crisp and brown outside and moist inside.

Ayam Bakar with Chilli

(Illustrated on p. 84)

Cooking time: 6 minutes
Grilling time: 12 minutes

1 chicken, about 1 kg
2 tablespoons black soy sauce
3 *daun limau purut*, shredded
2 teaspoons sugar
¼ teaspoon salt
4 tablespoons oil
1 large onion, sliced
2 tablespoons tamarind powder
200 millilitres water
1 tablespoon oil
1 stalk lemon grass, bruised

Rempah
2 large onions
2 cloves garlic
6 dried chillies
4 candlenuts

Wash and quarter chicken and marinate in soy sauce, *daun limau purut*, sugar and a little salt.

Heat oil and fry sliced onion till soft. Add *rempah* and fry till fragrant, then stir in tamarind mixed with water. Simmer for 3 minutes and remove *sambal* to cool.

Grill chicken pieces for 6 minutes on each side under a hot grill. Mix marinade with 1 tablespoon oil and baste chicken using bruised lemon grass. When chicken is cooked, spoon *sambal* over pieces and serve.

Grilled Spiced Spring Chicken

Grilling time: 20 minutes

1 tablespoon barbecue spice (a Spices of
   the Orient product)
2 spring chickens, about 250 g each
1 teaspoon salt
5 tablespoons water
3 tablespoons oil

Rempah
5 shallots
1 teaspoon ground turmeric
½ teaspoon chilli powder
1 teaspoon *belacan* powder
1 teaspoon black pepper
2 teaspoons ground coriander

Mix *rempah* with barbecue spice and rub this all over chickens. Leave to marinate for several hours or overnight.

Heat grill. Sprinkle salt on chickens and put on an oiled wire rack in a roasting pan. Put water in roasting pan to prevent burning from dripping oil when you baste. Grill for 15 or 20 minutes, basting with oil. Turn once or twice and test with a sharp skewer to see if chicken is cooked. If bloody liquid oozes out when you poke skewer in the thickest part of the thigh, chicken is not ready. If skewer comes out dry, chicken should be cooked. It's all a matter of taste. Personally, I like my chicken just done with a little raw marrow left.

Fried Chicken with Ginger and Pepper

Cooking time: 10 minutes

3 chicken drumsticks or 1 chicken breast
4 tablespoons oil
5 cm piece ginger, cut into fine strips
2 teaspoons black pepper
1 teaspoon salt
1 teaspoon sugar
2 teaspoons black soy sauce

Cut chicken into bite-sized pieces and dry thoroughly with absorbent paper. In a dry non-stick pan, fry chicken pieces until almost all moisture has evaporated and chicken is slightly crisp.

Remove chicken and put in oil. Fry ginger in oil until light brown. Add chicken and fry for 5 minutes. Add pepper, salt and sugar and continue frying until chicken is cooked. Sprinkle on a few drops of water if chicken is too dry. If you use a non-stick pan, this is not necessary.

Add soy sauce last and stir well to give chicken an overall dark colour. Stored in an airtight bottle, this can be kept for a few days.

Ayam Lemak Putih

Cooking time: 15 minutes
Grilling time: 5 minutes

This is an unusual curry in that no chilli is used yet it has a bite to it with the use of blended curry powder ingredients. There are two steps, boiling and grilling, but you can omit the second if you are rushed for time.

1 whole chicken, about 1 kg
1 coconut, grated
800 millilitres water
5 tablespoons oil
1 teaspoon salt
1 stalk lemon grass, bruised
2 slices galingale
1 tablespoon fish sauce

Rempah
1 large onion
3 cloves garlic
1 tablespoon ground cummin
1 tablespoon ground aniseed
3 tablespoons ground coriander

Wash chicken and remove giblets if you buy pre-packed fowl. Leave chicken whole. Squeeze coconut with water for milk. Blend *rempah* with 3 tablespoons coconut milk to make a paste.

Fry *rempah* in hot oil until fragrant and add whole chicken to fry until surface is well coated with *rempah*. Add coconut milk, salt, lemon grass, galingale and fish sauce and bring to a boil. Simmer for 15 minutes, turning chicken over once or twice.

Heat grill and place whole chicken in roasting pan under it. Grill for 5 minutes or until breast skin turns crisp. Serve with bread or plain rice and a side dip of plain black soy sauce.

Chicken and Bamboo Shoot Curry

Cooking time: 25 minutes

2 chicken breasts
2 pieces tinned bamboo shoot
3 tablespoons dried prawns
1 coconut, grated
750 millilitres water
4 tablespoons oil
1 teaspoon salt

Rempah
1 large onion
8 dried chillies
4 candlenuts
1 teaspoon galingale powder
2 teaspoons *belacan* powder
2 tablespoons ground coriander

Cut chicken into bite-sized pieces. Cut bamboo shoot into thin slices. Soak dried prawns in hot water and pound till fine. Squeeze coconut with water for milk.

Fry *rempah* in oil until fragrant and add coconut milk. Bring to a boil and add all other ingredients. Simmer for 20 minutes until oil rises to the top.

Chicken Kurmah

Cooking time: 40 minutes

1 coconut, grated
1 litre water
100 millilitres evaporated milk
3 tablespoons almonds, blanched, skinned and pounded
juice of 2 limes
3 large potatoes
1 chicken, about 1½ kg
2 teaspoons salt
4 tablespoons ghee
6 shallots, sliced fine
3 cm piece ginger, shredded
4 cm cinnamon stick
2 cardamoms
3 cloves
1 stalk lemon grass, bruised

Kurmah Paste
Use 6 tablespoons prepared *kurmah* powder (a Spices of the Orient product) moistened with 6 tablespoons water, or a blend of the following ingredients:
2 cloves garlic
6 candlenuts
2 tablespoons ground coriander
1 tablespoon ground cummin
1 tablespoon ground aniseed
2 teaspoons pepper

Squeeze coconut with water for coconut milk and mix 200 millilitres coconut milk with evaporated milk. Stir pounded almonds into this mixture and add lime juice. Leave mixture for 10 minutes to curdle.

Peel and quarter potatoes. Cut chicken into large joints and rub with salt to clean slime. Wash and drain.

Heat ghee and fry sliced shallots, ginger, cinnamon, cardamoms, cloves and lemon grass for 1 minute. Add *kurmah* paste and fry until fragrant and oil seeps out again. Add chicken joints and fry for a further 2 minutes. Add all other ingredients including coconut milk and coconut milk mixed with evaporated milk, almonds and lime juice. Simmer for 30 minutes. Serve with crusty French bread.

Roast Chicken in Coconut Milk

(Illustrated on p. 82)

Cooking time: 20 minutes
Grilling time: 10 minutes

1 chicken, about 1½ kg
½ coconut, grated
500 millilitres water
5 tablespoons oil
3 *daun limau purut*
1 teaspoon *laksa* leaf powder
2 *bunga siantan* (wild ginger flower)
   leaves
1 teaspoon salt

Rempah
3 dried chillies
1 stalk lemon grass
2 slices galingale or 1 teaspoon galingale
   powder
3 candlenuts
1 large onion
½ teaspoon ground turmeric
1 tablespoon ground coriander
1 teaspoon ground cummin
1 teaspoon ground aniseed

Wash chicken and leave whole, removing only claws. Squeeze coconut with water for milk.

Fry *rempah* in oil until fragrant. Add *daun limau purut*, *laksa* leaf powder and *bunga siantan* leaves and fry for 30 seconds. Add coconut milk and salt and bring to a boil. Put in chicken to simmer for 15 minutes. Liquid should have reduced to 300 millilitres by then.

Turn oven grill to high (Gas Mark 4). Remove chicken from gravy and place in a roasting tin. Put 200 millilitres of the gravy into the tin and reserve the rest for basting. Grill chicken for 10 minutes, turning occasionally to brown evenly. Baste occasionally so chicken is moist but with brown bits here and there. Serve chicken whole with gravy on the side or poured over chicken.

Chicken Tempera

Cooking time: 8 minutes

2 chicken drumsticks
3 chicken wings
1 tablespoon black soy sauce
2 teaspoons light fish sauce
1 tablespoon vinegar
1 teaspoon *belacan* powder
200 millilitres water
2 teaspoons sugar
4 tablespoons oil

Ingredients to be Sliced
2 red chillies
1 large onion
3 cloves garlic
1 stalk lemon grass
3 cm piece ginger
2 *daun limau purut*

Cut chicken into bite-sized pieces. Marinate in a mixture of soy sauce, fish sauce, vinegar, *belacan* powder, water and sugar. Leave for 30 minutes and drain, reserving marinade.

Heat oil and fry sliced ingredients for 30 seconds. Add chicken pieces and fry for a further 3 minutes. Add reserved marinade and simmer gently for 5 minutes. Adjust seasoning, adding more sugar, vinegar or soy sauce as your taste requires.

Spicy Fried Chicken

Cooking time: 10 minutes

1 chicken, about 1 kg
3 tablespoons tamarind powder
200 millilitres water
3 tablespoons oil
1 teaspoon salt
1 teaspoon sugar

Rempah
3 red chillies
1 large onion
2 cloves garlic
2 candlenuts

Cut chicken into chunks and marinate in tamarind mixed with water. Heat oil and fry *rempah* until oil seeps out again. Drain chicken chunks, reserving marinade, and fry in spices for 2 minutes.

Add reserved marinade a little at a time and continue to stir-fry until gravy is reduced. Add salt and sugar last and stir-fry about 5 minutes to finish cooking.

Chicken Liver with Pineapple

(Illustrated on p. 104)

Cooking time: 8 minutes

6 chicken livers
1 small pineapple
4 tablespoons oil
2 green chillies, sliced into three
1 teaspoon salt
100 millilitres water
2 teaspoons cornflour ⎫
3 tablespoons water ⎬ *mixed*

Boil chicken livers, then slice each into two. Quarter pineapple lengthwise, then cut each length diagonally into 1 cm thick slices.

Heat oil and fry green chillies till they shrink. Add pineapple pieces and fry for 2 minutes. Add chicken livers, salt and water and bring to a boil. Stir in cornflour mixture and when gravy thickens, turn off heat. Serve hot.

Chicken Curry

(Illustrated on pp. 18, 103)

Cooking time: 30 minutes

1 chicken, about 1 kg
1 teaspoon salt
3 large potatoes
1 large onion
1 piece ginger, about 3 × 2 cm
1 coconut, grated
1 litre water
4 tablespoons oil
3 tablespoons meat curry paste (p. 15)
1 teaspoon salt
1 teaspoon sugar

Cut chicken into large joints, discarding head and claws. Rub with a little salt and leave aside. Peel and quarter potatoes. Pound onion and ginger separately. Squeeze coconut with water for milk.

Fry onion and ginger in oil for 1 minute and add curry paste. Add chicken pieces and fry for a further 2 minutes until they are well coated. Add coconut milk and bring to a boil. Add potatoes, salt and sugar and simmer for 25 minutes.

Itek Sio

Cooking time: 1½ hours

Deceptively simple, this classic Nonya duck dish requires assiduous watching over the kwali *as it simmers to glazed perfection. Using an ordinary* kwali *over a gas flame or an electric range does not produce the same results as the old-fashioned method of simmering over charcoal. Since this is not practical, I cannot emphasize enough the importance of a non-stick utensil.*

The traditional sweetening agent that my mother and her mother before her used to add was sugar-cane. This is not always available, so sugar has to suffice, though the characteristic cane sugar fragrance is not present. But what is important about Itek Sio is the glaze. My aunts (the ones who were really great cooks) would sniff if someone in the house attempted this dish and did not come up with the required appearance that Itek Sio should have.

1 whole duck, about 2 kg, with head left on
3 tablespoons ground coriander, dry-fried over low heat until fragrant
2 teaspoons pepper
2 tablespoons sugar
2 teaspoons salt
4 tablespoons thick black soy sauce
4 tablespoons oil
20 shallots, sliced fine or pounded
2 litres water, more required if gravy dries up during simmering
5 cm stick cinnamon
6 cloves
1 bunch coriander leaves
2 stalks spring onions

Clean duck thoroughly, making sure insides are free of blood and traces of offal. Wipe dry with kitchen paper and rub duck all over with coriander, pepper, sugar, salt and soy sauce. Leave to marinate for at least 1 hour for the spices to soak in.

Put oil in pan (it is advisable to use a non-stick *kwali* with a lid) and fry shallots until light brown but not burnt. Put in duck and fry, turning constantly till every inch of skin is brown. The reason for using a non-stick pan is obvious. You get an evenly browned skin without burning.

When duck is well sizzled, add water, cinnamon and cloves and simmer. It is important, while duck is simmering, to keep turning it and spooning simmering gravy over all parts of the surface. It takes about an hour if you cover the *kwali* from time to time for about 5 minutes each time so the compressed steam cooks the duck faster. But this does not give the attractive glaze that comes from really slow simmering, with your hand never leaving the end of your wooden spoon.

Chop coriander leaves. Cut spring onions into 4 cm lengths and slit at both ends to resemble flower petals. Soak in ice-cold water.

Serve duck whole and let diners cut and come again as they wish. Garnish with coriander leaves and spring onions.

OPPOSITE: Itek Sio (recipe above).
PAGE 82: Roast Chicken in Coconut Milk (recipe p. 78).
PAGE 83: Braised Duck with Chestnuts, Dried Oysters and Liver Stuffing (recipe p. 143).
PAGE 84: Left to right, Ayam Bakar with Chilli (recipe p. 75) and Sambal Telur (recipe p. 100).

Vegetables

Though vegetable dishes usually appeared in co-starring roles on the Straitsborn dinner table, they were nevertheless cooked with as much tender loving care as were seafood and meat. The humble water convolvulus (*kangkung*) took on wondrous guises under the expert hands of Nonyas, spices added not in the least masking its natural goodness but enhancing every crunchy mouthful. And when left raw to be eaten in an *ulam* meal, vegetables were treated with reverence.

Not for the Straitsborn sorry-looking spinach or boiled-to-death cabbage. The classic *acar*, for instance, is a superb way to cook vegetables in spices without losing any of their nutrients. Lightly scalded and left to steep in an artful blend of turmeric, chilli, shallots and ginger, they best exemplify skilful Nonya vegetable cookery. None was ever regarded as lowly. Each had its place in the order of things. If fried at all, they would be in a *kwali* no longer than necessary to just cook them. In a dish like Sayur Lodeh, they would be boiled to just the right degree of doneness that wouldn't wait for you and I. And long before modern-day nutritionists decreed that vegetables were best left as raw as possible, I had the privilege of eating them so—in burning-hot Rojak, in *ulam* feasts and as garnishes for Mee Siam, Laksa and the multitude of spicy dishes that called for some vegetable or other to add the right fillip.

Think how poor our culinary heritage would be but for the Straitsborn ingenuity to cook such esoteric things like raw jackfruit, the bud and flowers of the banana plant, wild pods like *buah petai* and *buah jering*, and onions and garlic that would normally be ground for spices left unashamedly whole in *acar*.

How to Serve an Ulam Meal

(Illustrated on p. 20)

Of all the Nonya traditions, this one must be the most appetising with its roots at earthy levels. It was the custom to eat a meal sitting on mats on the floor and using no implements other than the plates on which the delicious array of sambals and raw vegetables were served. One used the fingers to scoop up as much rice and fish or meat or sambal as one wished, concocting a mix of flavours with each mouthful that was different from the next. An ulam (salad) meal used the simplest of ingredients, most grown in the backyard as I remember, with only fried fish as the foil for the tangy sambals. But that had to be parang (wolf herring) and nothing else. Next came plain boiled rice, fluffy and piping hot. The rest was an exercise in inventiveness. It was in this way that I learnt much about compatible flavours of certain vegetables and spices. An ulam meal is really what you make of it, given the basics like rice, fried fish, sambal belacan (a must) and crisp or boiled greens.

The classics are:

A large head of cabbage soaked in water for at least an hour

Fillets of *parang* (wolf herring) fried till crisp

Sambal belacan

***Buah petai* (green pods sold at Kandang Kerbau Market)**

***Buah jering* (yellow pods encased in black skins)**

Raw cucumber

Fresh green chillies

Chin char loke*/Prawn paste/Pounded *hae bee

Pickled cuttlefish (Hokkien: *kow nee koey*)

There are many garden-grown herbs that I used to eat as a child but since these are all but gone, I suggest using substitutes like watercress, English celery, courgettes, boiled lady's fingers, boiled brinjals, pineapple chunks and fried *bilis* (anchovy).

Cabbage

Simply wash and tear into large pieces. Eat with *sambal belacan* mashed with fried *parang*.

Parang (Wolf Herring)

Wash with salt and fry in hot oil for 5 minutes each side. Fry the roe separately and eat this with just a squeeze of lime juice and *sambal belacan*.

Sambal Belacan   (Illustrated on p. 18)

Toast 2 tablespoons of *belacan* paste over medium heat and pound with 5 red chillies and a pinch of salt. Sprinkle with a few drops of water if mixture is dry. Serve with lime juice mixed liberally in it. Remove lime pulp and cut lime skin to mix with *belacan*. This is a tangy and delicious way of eating *sambal belacan*.

Buah Petai

Remove seeds from pod and rub the thin skin off each seed. Leave in a bowl of clean water and eat with *sambal belacan* and fish.

Buah Jering

Remove yellow seeds from black pods and boil seeds in salt water for 20 minutes. I never found out why my mother used to put an enamel spoon in with the *jering* while they were boiling. It had something to do with removing toxic matter in the *jering* but there is no medical evidence that *jering* is poisonous. Eat as with *buah petai* or with grated coconut as a dessert.

Chin Char Loke   (Illustrated on p. 114)

These bottles of pickled *grago* (minute shrimps) are easily available at shops selling Penang foodstuffs and much nicer than if you were to make just a small amount at home. It's a very tricky thing to make and you either end up with fermented rice wine or terrible *chin char loke*. For this reason, I do not give the recipe. Good *chin char loke* must be pink in colour, does not have too strong a wine smell and is not too salty. The bottle must be kept tightly corked and refrigerated. Do not, under any circumstances, shake it before removing the contents. The cork will pop like a bullet from a gun as the gas build-up from the fermented rice has terrific driving force.

How to serve Chin Char Loke: Pour about 5 tablespoons onto a small dish. Cut 4 shallots fine. Slice 2 red and 2 green chillies fine. Slice about 1 tablespoon of young ginger fine. Cut skin of one lime (after squeezing out juice to mix with *chin char loke*) into small pieces and mix all together. Eat with fried *parang* (wolf herring) and rice.

Prawn Paste

There is nothing more simple than concocting a *sambal* with prawn paste. Simply mix 3 tablespoons prawn paste with 1 tablespoon *belacan*, lime juice from 2 limes and 1 tablespoon sugar and you have mouthwatering *sambal* to be eaten with sliced cucumber and pineapple. It is a simple form of Rojak, if you like. One other way to eat prawn paste is to dip fat, green chillies into the pure paste and eat as is. Tears will stream from your eyes if you are not accustomed to this kind of unadulterated zest.

Pounded Dried Prawns (Hokkien: *Hae Bee*)

Soak 5 tablespoons dried prawns in hot water and pound till fine. Mixed simply with *sambal belacan* (about 1 tablespoon) and 1 teaspoon sugar, it goes with all the vegetables mentioned.

Pickled Cuttlefish
(Hokkien: *Kow Nee Koey*)

These delightful mouthfuls of flavour used to be very common because fishermen who had extra catches of cuttlefish and not knowing what to do with them, pickled them in bottles much like *chin char loke*. Only a few shops sell them today but I get mine mostly from friends who return after visits to Malacca. If you can get a good bottle this is how to serve it with an *ulam* meal.

Remove about 5 cuttlefish and wash thoroughly under tap. Slice very fine and mix with finely sliced stem ginger, chillies and *daun limau purut*. This does not go with fried fish but just with plain rice. If cuttlefish is a little salty, counteract with 1 teaspoon vinegar.

Brinjals, Courgettes and Lady's Fingers

Boil these vegetables until just cooked (about 2 minutes in fast boiling water) and eat with any or a mixture of the *sambals* mentioned. You will find lady's fingers have natural affinity with prawn paste and *sambal belacan* and brinjals with fried fish and *sambal belacan*. Courgettes or baby marrows are really a western vegetable but just as delicious in *ulam*.

Jaganan

Cooking time: 15 minutes

This is a favourite Nonya salad which is a meal in itself.

200 g water convolvulus
¼ cabbage
10 long beans
200 g beansprouts
2 firm soybean cakes
    (Hokkien: *taukwa*)
2 tablespoons oil
2 hardboiled eggs
1 cucumber
prawn crackers (*kropok*)

Gravy
10 dried chillies
1 tablespoon *belacan* powder
10 shallots
10 pieces peanut brittle (Cantonese:
    fa sang tong), available at most
    coffee shops
600 millilitres water
3 tablespoons tamarind powder
1 teaspoon salt

Scald water convolvulus for 2 minutes and make little bundles with each stalk. Cut cabbage and long beans into serving sizes and scald for 1 minute. Scald beansprouts for 30 seconds.

Fry soybean cakes in oil until light brown, then quarter and cut into 1 cm thick slices. Slice hard-boiled eggs and cucumber.

Arrange all these ingredients on a large plate. Pour gravy over vegetables and garnish with prawn crackers (*kropok*).

Gravy
Soak dried chillies in hot water for 2 minutes and pound with *belacan* and shallots. Pound peanut brittle separately until fine.

Mix water with tamarind and bring to a boil. Add all pounded ingredients and salt and simmer for 5 minutes. If gravy is too thin, add more pounded brittle. (Peanut butter is a good substitute.)

Angled Loofah, Carrot and Egg Omelette

Cooking time: 3 minutes

1 angled loofah (Cantonese: *chi kuah*)
½ teaspoon salt
1 carrot
3 eggs
1 teaspoon fish sauce
½ teaspoon pepper
100 g small prawns
4 tablespoons oil
1 bunch coriander leaves

Skin angled loofah and remove soft centre. Cut into 1 cm thick strips and sprinkle with a little salt. Cut carrot into fine strips, wash and drain. Beat eggs in a bowl and season with fish sauce and pepper. Wash and peel prawns. Squeeze moisture out of angled loofah.

Heat oil until smoking and fry angled loofah and carrot very quickly for 1 minute. Pour egg mixture in and swirl the *kwali* if you are using one instead of a flat-bottomed pan. Sprinkle prawns all over egg mixture, spreading them evenly. After 1 minute, turn over and brown. Cut up omelette into rough pieces and serve garnished with fresh coriander leaves.

Hot Vegetable Curry

Cooking time: 10 minutes

6 lady's fingers
1 brinjal
2 tomatoes
1 carrot
4 green chillies
2 red chillies
2 tablespoons tamarind powder
350 millilitres water
½ coconut, grated
250 millilitres water
5 tablespoons oil
1 large onion, sliced
2 cloves garlic, crushed
1 sprig curry leaves
2 teaspoons salt
1 teaspoon sugar

Rempah
2 tablespoons ground coriander
1 teaspoon ground cummin
1 teaspoon ground aniseed
2 teaspoons chilli powder

Wash vegetables. Top and tail lady's fingers. Cut brinjal into two lengthwise. Halve tomatoes and cut carrot into chunks. Leave chillies whole. Mix tamarind powder with 350 millilitres water. Squeeze coconut with 250 millilitres water for milk.

Heat oil and fry sliced onion and crushed garlic until soft. Add *rempah* and fry until fragrant. Add curry leaves and fry for 1 minute, then add both tamarind and coconut liquids. Bring to a boil and put in carrot, brinjal, salt and sugar. Simmer for 4 minutes. Then add lady's fingers, tomatoes and chillies to simmer for 3 minutes. Lady's fingers should still have a crunch to them.

Long Beans in Dry Spices

Cooking time: 10 minutes

5 tablespoons oil
200 g belly pork, sliced thin
10 long beans, cut into 4 cm
   lengths
1 tablespoon sugar
2 teaspoons black soy sauce

Rempah
4 candlenuts
5 dried chillies
2 large onions
3 cloves garlic
1 teaspoon lemon grass powder
1 teaspoon galingale powder
1 teaspoon *belacan* powder
1 tablespoon water (use if
   required)

If *rempah* is too dry, add 1 tablespoon water to make it into a paste for easier frying.

Heat oil and fry *rempah* until fragrant. Add pork slices and fry for 2 minutes. Add long beans and continue frying for 8 minutes, stirring all the time until everything is well mixed and ingredients are cooked. Add sugar and soy sauce. Do not add water, even if *rempah* sticks a little. Just lower heat and stir-fry.

Nangka Lemak
(Jackfruit Curry)

Cooking time: 20 minutes

1 kg unripe jackfruit
1 teaspoon salt
1 coconut, grated
1.5 litres water
5 tablespoons oil
4 tablespoons dried prawns,
   soaked in water for a few
   minutes, then pounded
2 stalks lemon grass, bruised
300 g small prawns, shelled
1 teaspoon salt

Rempah
4 red chillies
3 candlenuts
2 large onions
1 tablespoon *belacan* powder
1 teaspoon ground turmeric

Cut off thick skin of jackfruit as close to the fibrous meat as possible. Cut into thick wedges, seeds and all, and soak in water. Boil a large pot of water, add 1 teaspoon salt and boil jackfruit for 20 minutes to soften and get rid of all sap. Drain.

Squeeze coconut with 1.5 litres water for milk.

Heat oil and fry dried prawns for 2 minutes. Add *rempah* and bruised lemon grass and fry for 2 minutes more until oil seeps out again. Add coconut milk and bring to a boil. Add jackfruit and simmer for 10 minutes, then put in shelled prawns and salt. Boil for 2 minutes more and serve hot.

Egg and Kiam Chye Omelette

Cooking time: 4 minutes

100 g small prawns
2 eggs
½ teaspoon salt
100 g salted vegetable
(Hokkien: *kiam chye*)
4 tablespoons oil
2 red chillies, sliced
1 sprig coriander leaves or
Chinese parsley

Wash and peel prawns. Beat eggs lightly with salt. Cut *kiam chye* into strips and soak in water for 5 minutes. Squeeze dry.

Heat oil and fry *kiam chye* for 1 minute. Add chillies and eggs and swirl pan to form a round omelette. Before top of egg mixture is cooked, add shelled prawns and cook for 2 minutes. Turn omelette over and cook through.

Cut up roughly with ladle and serve with coriander leaves or Chinese parsley.

Brinjals with Sambal Udang Kering

Cooking time: 8 minutes

2 brinjals
6 tablespoons dried prawns
3 tablespoons oil
1 large onion, sliced
1 teaspoon sugar
½ teaspoon salt
100 millilitres water
1 lime

Rempah
2 red chillies
6 shallots
2 candlenuts
1 teaspoon *belacan* powder

Cut stalks off brinjals, halve lengthwise and slice each half into 1 cm thick pieces. Soak in water while you are preparing other ingredients so brinjals do not turn black. Boil a little water and blanch brinjals for 2 minutes until they are half-cooked. (This is so you do not have to fry brinjals in oil for too long; frying tends to shrink them.)

Soak dried prawns in hot water for 3 minutes and wash well. Pound.

Drain brinjals and fry in very hot oil for 2 minutes. Lift up with a slotted spoon and leave aside.

In the same oil fry sliced onion until soft but not brown. Add *rempah* and dried prawns and fry over low heat. Dried prawns soak up oil, but after slow frying oil will seep out again. Add sugar, salt and water, a little at a time, until you get the required consistency. It should be thick.

Arrange brinjals on a dish and spoon fried *rempah* on top. Squeeze lime juice over it just before serving.

For an easier-to-prepare dish, cut brinjals into wedges. After spices have been fried, put in brinjal pieces and stir-fry for 2 minutes. Add water, sugar and salt and serve on top of plain rice.

Fried Chye Poh and Long Bean Sambal

Cooking time: 4 minutes

2 pieces preserved radish
  (Hokkien: *chye poh*)
4 tablespoons oil
1 firm soybean cake
6 long beans
2 cloves garlic, crushed
2 tablespoons sugar
2 red or green chillies,
  sliced
1 lime

Soak *chye poh* in water for 10 minutes and then chop fine. (You can also chop first before soaking.) Squeeze out water to rid it of excess salt.

In a non-stick pan, heat 2 tablespoons oil and fry soybean cake until brown. When cold, dice into fine cubes. Dice long beans fine.

Add remaining oil to the *kwali* or pan and fry crushed garlic until brown. Squeeze *chye poh* until completely dry and fry until fragrant. Add long beans and soybean cake and continue frying for 3 minutes until cooked and beans are slightly brown. Add sugar and chillies and stir-fry for a few minutes more.

By now the combination of chilli, sugar and garlic should be sending you into a sneezing fit, which means the *sambal* is ready. To serve, squeeze the juice of one lime over. It makes a very nice relish to be eaten with hot rice.

Lady's Fingers with Prawn Sambal

Cooking time: 8 minutes

10 lady's fingers
3 tablespoons oil
100 g small prawns, shelled
350 millilitres water
1 teaspoon salt

Rempah
3 candlenuts
6 shallots
2 cloves garlic
1 teaspoon *belacan* powder
1 teaspoon chilli powder

Cut lady's fingers diagonally into bite-sized pieces, wash and drain. Scald very quickly in hot water to remove some of the slime.

Heat oil and fry *rempah* until fragrant. Add lady's fingers and prawns and fry for 2 minutes. Add water and salt and simmer for 5 minutes until liquid is reduced by half.

Koo Chye Flowers with Taukwa

Cooking time: 5 minutes

150 g flowers of Chinese chives
   (Hokkien: *koo chye huey*)
150 g small prawns
3 tablespoons oil
2 firm soybean cakes (Hokkien:
   ***taukwa*)**
1 clove garlic, crushed
150 millilitres water
1 teaspoon salt
a pinch of monosodium glutamate

Cut *koo chye* into 4 cm lengths and wash well. Wash and shell prawns, removing green vein.

Heat oil in a *kwali* and fry soybean cakes for a few minutes. Remove and cut into small pieces. In remaining oil, saute crushed garlic for 1 minute and add *koo chye*. Fry over high heat for 2 minutes and add prawns and soybean cakes. Add water, salt and monosodium glutamate and simmer for 1 minute.

Sayur Lodeh
(Lontong Gravy)

Cooking time: 15 minutes

½ cabbage
15 French beans
½ turnip
1 coconut, grated
1.5 litres water
4 tablespoons oil
2 slices galingale
2 tablespoons dried prawns,
   soaked in water, then pounded
200 g small prawns, shelled
4 firm soybean cakes (Hokkien: *taukwa*),
   cut into triangles
1 teaspoon salt

Rempah
4 candlenuts
10 shallots
2 cloves garlic
6 dried chillies or
   1 teaspoon chilli powder
1 teaspoon ground turmeric
1 teaspoon ground coriander
1 tablespoon *belacan* powder

Cut cabbage and French beans into bite-sized pieces. Skin turnip and cut into strips about 4 cm long and 1 cm thick. Squeeze coconut with water for milk (you should get more than 1.5 litres).

Fry *rempah* in oil until fragrant and add galingale slices and dried prawns. Add coconut milk and bring to a boil. Add all other ingredients and simmer for 10 minutes.

This is traditionally served with rice cakes, the recipe for which is given opposite. Served with plain boiled rice, Lontong is just as delicious.

Lontong Rice Cakes

Cooking time: 15 minutes

500 g broken rice
1.5 litres water
pinch of salt

Wash rice and put to boil with water and salt, stirring occasionally to break up broken rice grains even further. Use an electric rice cooker or an asbestos mat under your ordinary rice pot to prevent burning. Let rice dry completely. Its consistency should be soft and like very thick porridge.

Transfer rice into a wide-mouthed pot and put a plate on top to fit just nicely. Weight this with a heavy object or your pestle and mortar. The plate should be of slightly smaller circumference than the pot so every part of the rice is weighted down.

Ideally, *lontong* rice should be cooked the day before and left weighted down in the refrigerator. Cut into 4 x 2 cm pieces and serve with Lontong gravy.

Vegetable Lemak with Sweet Potatoes

Cooking time: 12 minutes

The classic vegetable for this dish is sayur paki but this has vanished from the scene. Spinach and water convolvulus make decent substitutes.

100 g spinach
100 g water convolvulus
2 small sweet potatoes
1 tablespoon dried prawns
1 coconut, grated
800 millilitres water
4 tablespoons oil
1 teaspoon salt

Rempah
1 large onion
8 dried chillies
2 teaspoons *belacan* powder
1 teaspoon ground turmeric

Wash and cut vegetables into bite-sized stalks and drain. Do not leave to soak in water as the nutrients will be washed away. Skin sweet potatoes and cut into large chunks. Pound dried prawns fine after soaking in hot water for a few minutes. Squeeze coconut with 800 millilitres water to obtain about 1 litre coconut milk.

Heat oil and fry *rempah* until fragrant. Add dried prawns and fry for a few more minutes. Add coconut milk and bring to a boil. Add sweet potatoes and simmer for 5 minutes, then add vegetables and salt.

Homemade Rojak

Cooking and Preparation time: 5 minutes

If you happen to have one of those glazed earthenware pots, which the rojak *hawker uses to grind and mix his* rojak *ingredients, and the wooden grinder, it's fun to entertain guests by preparing it at the table after all the ingredients have been prepared. Otherwise, any wide-mouthed mixing bowl and a wooden spoon will do just as well.*

150 g beansprouts, tailed and scalded
    for 20 seconds
1 small turnip, cut into slivers
2 pieces pineapple, cut into wedges
1 large cucumber, cut into wedges
200 g water convolvulus, plucked
    into 5 cm lengths and scalded
    for 1 minute
1 medium-sized sweet potato, cut into
    thin slices
1 green mango, cut into slivers
2 or 3 crullers (Hokkien: *yu char kway*),
    cut into pieces
2 dried soybean cakes (Hokkien: *tau pok*),
    cut into pieces
1 *bunga siantan* (wild ginger flower),
    thinly sliced
2 limes (optional)

Grind Together for Rojak Sauce:
3 dried chillies or 4 *chilli padi*
    (bird chillies)
1 tablespoon toasted *belacan* paste
2 tablespoons prawn paste (Hokkien:
    hayko)
2 tablespoons white or palm sugar
5 tablespoons pounded roasted
    peanuts
4 tablespoons tamarind powder mixed
    with 325 millilitres water and boiled

(Use 5 pieces peanut brittle, *fa sang tong* in Cantonese, pounded, to substitute for sugar and peanuts)

Mix all ingredients (except *bunga siantan*, limes and a few tablespoons pounded peanut brittle or peanuts) well. If you like a tangy taste to your *rojak*, squeeze the juice of 2 limes over it. Serve garnished with pounded peanuts or peanut brittle and grated *bunga siantan*.

Jantong Pisang
(Banana Bud Sambal with
Prawns and Coconut Cream)

(Illustrated on p. 101)

Cooking time: 10 minutes

1 large *jantong pisang* (banana bud),
  or 2 small ones
1 litre water
1 coconut, grated
125 millilitres water
2 teaspoons salt
400 g small prawns, boiled and
  shelled
15 *belimbing buloh* (sour star
  fruit), sliced diagonally
2 tablespoons *sambal belacan*
  (p. 86), or pound 4 red chillies
  with 2 tablespoons toasted
  belacan paste
juice of 2 limes
1 teaspoon sugar

Preparing banana buds is a laborious process but the results are worth your effort. Peel off each layer of the purple skin and remove pale yellow flowers, keeping them immersed in water so they do not turn black. Repeat until you reach the tender heart of the bud. Cut this centre into small pieces.

Now comes the difficult part. In each and every single flower is a hard stamen that looks like a hooked needle. Remove this. (There is no other way but by doing it one by one.) Boil the flowers and heart in 1 litre water for 3 minutes. Remove and drain to cool.

Squeeze coconut with 125 millilitres water for coconut cream. Bring the coconut cream with salt to a slow boil in a non-stick pot, stirring all the time until it thickens a little. To serve, mix all ingredients together. This *sambal* is best eaten slightly chilled.

Sambals and Special Dishes

Of all the dishes in Straitsborn cuisine, few—indeed, none—can quite match Popiah for taste and character that lend beautifully to gourmandising bonhomie. Quite a mouthful, this statement, but who has sat down to a Popiah meal and not thoroughly enjoyed making his own fat, thin, long or stumpy roll filled with goodness? For reasons of convenience, Popiah is generally referred to as a spring roll but it is much more than this. The plethora of ingredients are as much spice for conversation as the occasion on which you serve Popiah. It is not unlike an *ulam* meal where you take as much or as little of each ingredient as pleases you and roll up the delicious flavour in *popiah* skins. Thanks to the enterprising nature of a few Singaporeans, *popiah* skins are still easily available. They are near to impossible to make at home but, as a substitute, one could use mass-produced spring roll skins sold in packets. Popiah, when wrapped with these skins, have to be fried before they can be eaten.

What is also nice about preparing Popiah is its demands on the entire family's cutting, cooking and pounding skills. In these days of nuclear families, the occasion when someone decides to serve Popiah for a festive occasion is always looked forward to as an opportunity for far-flung family members to gather together under one roof and eat hearty. It is rarely ever prepared for fewer than, say, four people because it is meant to be enjoyed by many at one sitting. Still, if you love it enough you should not be put off by this, but make Popiah for one, two or four.

On the other end of the culinary scale, side dishes and *sambals* that never fail to appear on a Straitsborn table seem to be regarded as appetisers for one or two people. Yet, Nonya sambals are highlights—co-stars if you like—to the main dishes. Nonyas gave them as much care as they did grand dishes. They could be subtle, like fried coconut (Serondeng) or fiery, like the simple *chilli padi* sauce. They are as important to the whole as the period at the end of this sentence. The principle remains constant: a sharp or tart *sambal* to counteract an oily soup; a fragrant and crunchy fried Ikan Bilis to balance rich Nasi Lemak. And last but not least, what is a festive Nonya meal without Acar? Spicy, crunchy, tart and sweet, a compote of cucumber, carrot, cabbage, onions, cauliflower, garlic, fat green chillies stuffed with grated papaya and sesame seeds, it is the epitome of Nonya sambals, a star in its own right. Many a time have I eaten a meal of rice and Acar and not much else and felt a surfeit of burping proportions. There are pickles and pickles, but only Nonya Acar requires the painstaking preparation that makes it a side dish with up-front reputation.

I remember my grandmother, mother and aunts all pitching in to slice mountains of cucumbers to dry them in the sun, choosing shallots of exact size, laboriously shredding raw papaya hair-fine and endlessly pounding the large amounts of *rempah* that went into this magnificent pickle. Then they would scald the vegetables in good vinegar, squeeze them dry, fry them in *rempah* and make up huge pots that kept for months.

The Acar of my childhood did not have a single soggy vegetable nor did it curl your lips with tartness. The balance of flavours was always perfect and my grandmother would cast her beady eye on anyone who had the temerity to add a surreptitious teaspoon of sugar to her Acar—it is, after all, the greatest tribute to a cook when you eat a dish without adding any more seasoning to it.

Unlike in western cuisine, not a condiment appears on the Asian dining table, not a tired-looking green meant only for visual appeal, and not an implement as 'barbaric' as a knife to cut up food. This is not to cast aspersions on western cuisine, but Nonya and all Asian cooks regard cooking and carving as things which belong exclusively in the kitchen—which is why you rarely see hunks of beef and whole fowl on Asian tables.

Yong Taufu Lemak

Cooking time: 10–15 minutes

1 bittergourd
250 g fish meat
¼ teaspoon salt
2 dried soybean cakes (Hokkien: *tau pok*)
2 firm soybean cakes (Hokkien: *taukwa*)
1 coconut, grated
700 millilitres water
5 tablespoons oil
6 fishballs
2 teaspoons salt
2 teaspoons *laksa* leaf powder

Rempah
1 large onion
2 cloves garlic
3 candlenuts
1 teaspoon galingale powder
1 teaspoon lemon grass powder
1 teaspoon chilli powder
1 teaspoon ground turmeric

Wash and cut bittergourd into 1 cm thick slices after removing seeds. Mix fish meat with ¼ teaspoon salt. If you buy ready-prepared fish meat, do not add any salt as it is pre-salted.

Cut dried and firm soybean cakes into triangles and make a slit in the diagonal of each triangle. Stuff bittergourd and soybean triangles with fish meat.

Squeeze coconut with 700 millilitres water for milk.

Heat oil and fry stuffed ingredients for 2 minutes. Boil fishballs in water until they float to the surface. Remove.

In remaining oil fry *rempah* until fragrant and add coconut milk. Bring to a boil and add all ingredients except *laksa* leaf powder. Simmer for 5 minutes and add salt. Add *laksa* leaf powder just before serving.

Acar

(Illustrated on pp. 44, 102)

Cooking time: 30 minutes

**1 kg cucumbers, inside pith discarded,
cut into 4 cm strips**
400 g cabbage, cut into 5 x 5 cm pieces
**200 g carrots, cut into strips half the
thickness of cucumbers, but of same
length**
1 tablespoon salt
40 shallots of even size
20 cloves garlic of even size
**1 small cauliflower, about 500 g,
cut into flowerets**
**30 plump green chillies, seeded and
slit on one side to make cavity
for stuffing**
**10 pieces peanut brittle (Cantonese:
fa sang tong), available at most
coffee shops, pounded**
**4 tablespoons sesame seed, dry-fried
till golden brown**

Liquid for Scalding Vegetables
1 litre vinegar ⎤
1 tablespoon salt ⎦ *mixed*

Rempah for Vegetables
15 shallots
6 candlenuts
15 dried chillies
2 teaspoons ground turmeric
100 millilitres oil
150 g ginger, shredded fine
200 millilitres vinegar
200 g sugar

Rempah for Chillies
**½ small green papaya, grated
thread-fine**
4 tablespoons oil
3 candlenuts, pounded
½ large onion, pounded
1 teaspoon *belacan* powder
**10 g dried prawns, soaked in
water, then pounded**
2 teaspoons sugar
½ teaspoon salt

How to Prepare Vegetables
After washing all vegetables, use a cloth to
dry thoroughly. Sprinkle 1 tablespoon salt
on cucumbers, cabbage and carrots and
leave for 10 minutes before squeezing out as
much moisture as you can, through a muslin cloth, without breaking up vegetables.
The alternative is to dry them in the sun for
1 or 2 days, spread out on trays. You may
not have the time, but this time-consuming
method produces crunchy *acar*. It is not
necessary to squeeze out moisture from
shallots, garlic, cauliflower and chillies. Peel
shallots and garlic and wipe dry with a clean
cloth.

Bring the vinegar and salt mixture for
scalding vegetables to a boil and scald each
vegetable in batches for ¾ – 1 minute until all
are done. Remove with a perforated spoon.
Leave on a tray to cool. If vinegar takes on a
darkish hue, discard and start with a fresh
amount to scald the rest of the vegetables.

How to Prepare Rempah for Vegetables
Pound shallots, candlenuts and chillies till
fine and add ground turmeric. Heat 100
millilitres oil until smoking and fry shredded
ginger until light brown. Add pounded ingredients and fry until oil seeps out again.
Add 200 millilitres vinegar and 200 g sugar
and stir well. Set aside and leave to cool.

How to Prepare Chillies
If you can, dry raw papaya shreds in the sun
for half a day or so until dry. Heat 4 tablespoons oil in a *kwali* and fry pounded
candlenuts, onion and *belacan* for 3
minutes, then add pounded dried prawns
and papaya shreds. Add sugar and salt and
stir well. Allow to cool. Stuff chillies firmly
with papaya *rempah*.

Put Them Together
Mix vegetables, stuffed chillies and *rempah*
for vegetables together in a pyrex or enamel
pot (never use aluminium as vinegar has a
chemical reaction with the metal, turning it
black and giving a peculiar metallic taste to
your *acar*). Either mix peanut brittle and
sesame seed with the mixture or add a little
of each when you serve the *acar*. Prepared
this way, with no water, *acar* can be kept
for weeks in the refrigerator.

Cucumber Pickle

This can be used as a pickle for Sweet Sour Fish or eaten by itself as a relish.

3 cucumbers
2 teaspoons salt
3 tablespoons malt vinegar
4 tablespoons sugar

Wipe cucumbers clean (do not wash) and skin. Cut into 4 lengthwise and remove central pith. Cut into diagonal pieces 1 cm thick and sprinkle with salt. Leave for 20 minutes and wrap cucumber pieces in muslin cloth. Gently squeeze out moisture and mix with vinegar and sugar. Let stand at least half an hour before serving.

Sambal Kuakchye

This is the dark green pickled vegetable you usually get with Babi Panggang.

1 kg *kuakchye* (Cantonese: *kai choy*)
3 teaspoons salt
150 g ginger
1 teaspoon salt
2 tablespoons sugar
4 tablespoons malt vinegar
3 teaspoons mustard

Slice *kuakchye* into thin strips and wash. Drain and mix well with 3 teaspoons salt. Leave for a few minutes and squeeze dry. Pound ginger roughly and mix with 1 teaspoon salt. Squeeze out ginger juice.

Mix all ingredients well and leave mixture to pickle in a glass or enamel container for at least 12 hours. It is traditionally served with Hati Babi Bungkus or Babi Panggang.

Quick Saltfish Sambal

Cooking time: 5 minutes

1 large piece *kurau* (threadfin) saltfish, about 6 × 5 cm
4 tablespoons oil
5 *chilli padi* (bird chilli)
2 limes
1 tablespoon sugar
4 shallots, sliced fine

Cut saltfish into strips and fry in hot oil until fragrant. Roughly chop *chilli padi* and mix with juice of two limes, sugar and sliced shallots. Add saltfish and serve as a *sambal*.

Saltfish Pickle

Cooking time: 15 minutes

We had the privilege of having Eurasian neighbours living on either side of our house for many years and if there is anyone who can make the best saltfish pickle, it's the Eurasian community. One of our neighbours had a family retainer who also learnt to cook very well and it was this lady who taught my mother how to do her sinfully delicious saltfish pickle. Anyone who has eaten good saltfish pickle will tell you what I mean.

400 g *kurau* (threadfin) saltfish (no other saltfish will do)
250 millilitres oil
6 cloves garlic, sliced fine
4 slices ginger, sliced fine
2 tablespoons sugar
3 tablespoons good vinegar (malt or wine, not artificial)
150 millilitres water
5 tablespoons sesame seeds, washed, drained and dry-fried

Rempah
15 shallots or 3 large Spanish onions
6 slices ginger
20 dried chillies
2 tablespoons ground coriander
1 tablespoon ground cummin
1 tablespoon ground aniseed

Cut saltfish into small pieces and fry in some of the oil until crisp and brown. Set aside.

Fry *rempah* in remaining hot oil until fragrant. Add sliced garlic and ginger and continue frying until *rempah* is well cooked and oil seeps out again. Add sugar, vinegar and water and stir-fry until almost dry. Add sesame seeds. Allow to cool and add saltfish pieces.

Store in a glass bottle (never metal) and serve small portions at a time as this is a strong pickle and an acquired taste.

Sambal Telur

(Illustrated on pp. 84, 103)

Cooking time: 15 minutes

4 tablespoons oil
1 tablespoon tamarind powder
300 millilitres water
1 teaspoon salt
1 teaspoon sugar
3 hardboiled eggs

Rempah
2 large onions
2 cloves garlic
3 candlenuts
6 dried chillies

Fry *rempah* in oil until fragrant. Add tamarind powder mixed with water, salt and sugar and simmer for 3 minutes. Put hardboiled eggs in to be coated with *sambal* and lift out. To serve, cut each egg into two and coat halves with sambal.

Note: You can also fry the hardboiled eggs in hot oil quickly till egg surface turns a crinkly light brown, before coating with *sambal*. They look more appetising this way.

OPPOSITE: Jantong Pisang (recipe p. 95).
PAGE 102: Acar (recipe p. 98).

Sambal Bendi Santan

Cooking time: 8 minutes

10 lady's fingers
1 coconut, grated
50 millilitres water
1 teaspoon salt
3 tablespoons dried prawns
1 tablespoon *sambal belacan* (p. 86)

Cut stalks off lady's fingers and boil in water for 2–4 minutes. The time depends on whether you like them crunchy or soft. Remove and drain under a running tap. Keep refrigerated. Squeeze coconut with water for milk.

In a small saucepan, boil coconut milk over low heat, stirring all the time until thick. Add salt. (A quicker way to thicken coconut milk is to add 1 tablespoon cornflour dissolved in a little water, but this adulterates the taste somewhat.) Remove from heat and allow to cool. Refrigerate.

Soak dried prawns in hot water and pound till fine. To serve, assemble all ingredients by pouring coconut milk over lady's fingers and mixing pounded dried prawns with *sambal belacan* before spooning this on top of the coconut milk. This *sambal* is best eaten chilled.

Leeks Fried with Prawns

Cooking time: 4 minutes

4 leeks
3 tablespoons oil
2 cloves garlic
150 g prawns, shelled
200 millilitres water
1 teaspoon salt
pinch of monosodium glutamate

Wash leeks, discard green ends and slice diagonally into 4 cm pieces. The reason for cutting vegetable diagonally is the maximum surface area gets sealed from high-heat stir-frying and vegetable remains crisp but cooked.

Heat oil and fry garlic until brown. Add leeks and stir-fry for 2 minutes. Add prawns and stir-fry for 1 minute more. Add water and seasoning and simmer for 2 minutes until leeks are soft.

PAGE 103: Left to right, Sambal Telur (recipe p. 100) and Chicken Curry (recipe p. 79).
OPPOSITE: Chicken Liver with Pineapple (recipe p. 79).

Chilli Padi Sauce with Lime

This is blazing hot so warn guests who may not be quite used to its mouth-burning property.

10 *chilli padi* **(bird chilli)**
4 tablespoons black soy sauce
1 tablespoon sugar
2 limes

Wash *chilli padi* (some people prefer to leave the stalks on for an ethnic touch) and crush roughly into soy sauce. Add sugar and squeeze lime juice over. Remove pulp and slice lime skin into slivers and mix well. Serve as a dip for baked or fried fish.

Kacang Goreng (Roasted Peanuts)

Cooking time: 25 minutes

I find it eminently useful to have a glass jar of homemade kacang goreng *(fried peanuts like the* kacang putih *man sells) as it can go into so many* sambal *sauces or be eaten as they are. It is a simple job requiring perhaps half an hour, but beware the skinning process! For this, it's ideal to have an open space below which there should not be anybody's drying laundry as the winnowing process, when removing peanut skin, can be a veritable 'skin storm'.*

1 kg raw peanuts with skin
1 level tablespoon rough salt or table salt

Heat a large *kwali* until metal begins to smoke and put raw peanuts and salt in to fry. Lower heat and stir-fry constantly for at least 20 minutes. There must be no compromise for this or you will end up with burnt peanuts that are raw inside. With a quick to-and-fro motion, much like frying *rempah*, stir-fry until peanut skin begins to blister and turn brown and black. Test by tasting one peanut.

Remove and place on a large flat tray. Allow to cool for at least 30 minutes so you can handle them without burning your palms. Fried peanuts hot from the pan can cause nasty burns. Rub handfuls of peanuts between your palms until all skin has been removed. Holding your tray in front of you, flick it up to winnow away skin. Repeat the rubbing and winnowing actions until all skin has been removed. Store peanuts in a glass bottle.

Fried Ikan Bilis with Peanuts in Chilli

Cooking time: 10 minutes

100 g dried *bilis* (anchovy)
3 tablespoons oil
3 dried chillies
1 clove garlic
2 tablespoons sugar
150 g roasted peanuts (p. 106)
1 tablespoon tamarind paste
50 millilitres water

Remove all foreign matter from *bilis* but do not wash or they will take ages to brown.

Heat oil and fry *bilis* for 3 or 4 minutes to brown until crisp. Remove with a slotted spoon and set aside.

Soak dried chillies in hot water until soft and pound till fine with garlic. Fry this chilli paste in hot oil for a few minutes and add sugar, stirring to prevent burning. Add peanuts, *bilis* and tamarind (mixed with water and strained) a little at a time till you have a moist consistency. It must not be watery and the sugar should have crystallised a little on contact with cold liquid. Cook for one or two minutes longer and dish up to serve with Nasi Lemak (p. 109) or use as a sandwich filling.

Pineapple Sambal with Belacan

Cooking time: 20 minutes

I'm not too sure of the origin of this side dish but one of my aunts used to prepare it and passed it on.

1 whole pineapple
2 tablespoons oil
200 millilitres water
4 tablespoons sugar
1 tablespoon *sambal belacan* (p. 86)
1 stalk lemon grass, bruised

Cut pineapple into fan-shaped pieces 1 cm thick. Remove core if you do not like its sharpness, but cooking tempers it a little. Heat oil and fry them quickly until well coated. Add water and simmer for 15 minutes over low heat until water has all but evaporated. Add sugar and continue simmering until sauce is lightly glazed. Add *sambal belacan* and finish cooking till almost dry, then add lemon grass.

It's a delicious tangy condiment that is best served chilled.

Sambal Nenas

1 cucumber
1 small pineapple
3 tablespoons dried prawns
3 red chillies
2 *daun limau purut*
2 teaspoons sugar

Skin cucumber, remove central pith and dice fine. Skin pineapple, remove hard core and dice slightly larger than cucumber. Soak dried prawns in hot water and pound till fine. Chop red chillies roughly and shred *daun limau purut* hair-fine.

Mix all ingredients and serve immediately. If you are preparing this *sambal* ahead, leave out the sugar until just before serving or it will become watery.

Note: Substitute chopped chilli with 1–2 tablespoons *sambal belacan* (p. 86) if you like it hot.

Sambal Serondeng
(Fried Coconut)

(Illustrated on p. 113)

Cooking time: 10 minutes

1 coconut, grated without skin
6 shallots, sliced fine
2 cloves garlic, sliced fine
1 piece *tempe* (fermented soybean cake), diced

In a dry pan, fry all ingredients for about 10 minutes. It is important to stir constantly so coconut browns evenly. Serve with Sayur Lodeh (p. 92) or Nasi Ketupat. The latter is compressed rice in coconut fronds specially woven to form packets. They are troublesome to make but can be ordered from most Satay stalls. A good substitute is Lontong Rice Cakes (p. 93).

Mango Sambal

3 green mangoes
1 teaspoon salt
5 red chillies
1 tablespoon *belacan* paste
1 tablespoon sugar

Grate green mangoes roughly and sprinkle with salt. Make *sambal belacan* in the usual way (see p. 86) and mix with grated mango. Add sugar and adjust seasoning to taste.

Nasi Lemak with Lauk Piring

Cooking time: 15 minutes

300 g rice
300 millilitres water
1 coconut, grated
500 millilitres water
1 teaspoon salt
2 *pandan* (screwpine) leaves

Wash rice in several changes of water and drain. Put rice and 300 millilitres water in a steaming tray.

Squeeze coconut with 500 millilitres water for milk. Mix coconut milk with salt and stir into rice, mixing well. Push *pandan* leaves into rice and steam for 15 minutes.

Serve Nasi Lemak accompanied with any of these Lauk Piring:
1 Ikan Pari Masak Pedas (p. 109)
2 Kangkung Lemak (p. 110)
3 Tamban Goreng Asam (p. 45)
4 Telur Goreng (p. 110)
5 Hot Sambal Goreng (p. 47)
6 Sliced Cucumber

Nonya Nasi Lemak with Lauk Piring bears little resemblance to the pre-packed ones sold at markets and, in some rural areas, by itinerant vendors. The coconut rice is basically the same but the range of Lauk Piring—literally in Malay, food for plates—is a magnificent extension of mere omelette, Sambal Ikan Bilis and cucumber slices. Nasi Lemak is a culinary tradition as rich as Popiah, Nasi Ulam and other similar Nonya meals built on several dishes and sambals.

Ikan Pari Masak Pedas

Cooking time: 12 minutes

2 tablespoons tamarind paste
500 millilitres water
400 g *pari* (ray fish), cut into 3 cm cubes
1 stalk lemon grass, bruised
1 teaspoon salt
1 teaspoon sugar

Rempah
2 candlenuts
3 red chillies
2 teaspoons galingale powder
1 teaspoon ground turmeric
1 tablespoon *belacan* powder

Squeeze tamarind with water. Strain. Put tamarind liquid to a boil and stir in *rempah*. Boil for 10 minutes to reduce a little and put in all other ingredients to boil for 2–3 minutes. Serve hot.

Kangkung Lemak

Cooking time: 8 minutes

300 g water convolvulus
200 g small prawns
½ coconut, grated
350 millilitres water
4 tablespoons oil
2 teaspoons salt

Rempah
3 candlenuts
1 large onion
2 cloves garlic
4 dried chillies
1 tablespoon *belacan* powder
1 teaspoon ground coriander
1 teaspoon ground turmeric

Wash vegetable thoroughly and cut into small stalks. Wash and shell prawns. Squeeze coconut with water for milk.

Heat oil and fry *rempah* till fragrant. Add coconut milk and salt and bring to a boil. Add vegetable and simmer till cooked, about 5 minutes. Add prawns last and simmer for 1 minute.

Telur Goreng

Cooking time: 3 minutes

3 eggs
¼ teaspoon salt
4 tablespoons oil

Beat eggs lightly and add salt. Heat oil in *kwali* and fry, swirling *kwali* to form a nice round of egg. Cook for 2 minutes on each side and lift to cool. Fold over twice and cut into triangles.

Sambal Babi with Chin Char Loke

(Illustrated on p. 114)

Cooking time: 20 minutes

500 g streaky pork with skin, in one piece
1 teaspoon salt
1 litre water
1 stalk lemon grass, bruised

Boil whole piece of pork for 20 minutes with salt in 1 litre water. Add lemon grass during last 10 minutes of boiling, after water has reduced a little. Lift pork out to cool and chill slightly. Slice thin and serve with *chin char loke* (p. 86).

Pork Skin and Cucumber Sambal

(Illustrated on p. 19, 114)

Cooking time: 45 minutes

1 large piece pork skin, about 15 cm
square
1 cucumber
3 tablespoons dried prawns
5 red chillies
7 cm square piece *belacan* paste, toasted
a little boiled water (use if necessary)
1 teaspoon sugar
4 limes

Boil pork skin for 45 minutes and leave to cool. Slice into bite-sized pieces. Cut away central pith of cucumber, slice lengthwise into four strips, then cut strips diagonally into bite-sized pieces. Soak dried prawns in hot water for 5 minutes and pound until fine.

Pound together red chillies and toasted *belacan* paste. Add a drop or two of boiled water if the *sambal belacan* is too dry.

Mix *sambal belacan*, dried prawns, pork skin and cucumber together and add sugar and lime juice to taste, a little at a time. For added zest cut lime skin into strips for garnish.

Popiah

Cooking time: 30 minutes

The nicest thing about eating homemade Popiah is you can add as much of this or that and create your own blend. If you have never attempted to make your own Popiah before, don't be daunted by the number of ingredients. The only cooking is the filling and the rest a matter of organised assembly. You do not have to stick strictly to all the ingredients (apart from the bamboo shoot filling of course) and Popiah sold by hawkers do not have half as many ingredients as homemade ones.

Here's an important tip. After buying popiah *(spring roll) skins, dampen a teacloth and cover skins to prevent from drying up. Do not fold* popiah *skin into quarters as they tend to crack at the folds when kept unused for a few hours. Use cling cellophane wrap to keep leftover skins and refrigerate for the next day.*

Filling
1 kg tinned bamboo shoots
1 sweet turnip
500 g belly pork
300 g small prawns

1 litre water
5 tablespoons oil
6 cloves garlic, crushed
4 tablespoons preserved soy beans
(Hokkien: *taucheo*), mashed
2 teaspoons salt

Other Ingredients
750 g *popiah* (spring roll) skin
3-4 stalks Chinese lettuce, washed and
dried thoroughly
600 g beansprouts, tailed and scalded for
1 minute
500 g small prawns, shelled and steamed
for 5 minutes
6 Chinese sausages (Cantonese: *lap
cheong*), steamed and sliced fine
3 firm soybean cakes (Hokkien: *taukwa*),
fried in 4 tablespoons oil and
shredded fine
2 crabs, steamed and meat extracted
4 hardboiled eggs, sliced fine
2 dried sole (Hokkien: *tikpo*), fried and
pounded fine
150 g roasted peanuts (p. 106), pounded
fine

Relishes
10 red chillies
4 dried, soaked chillies | *pounded fine*
1 or 2 bottles sweet sauce (look for 'flour sauce' and not the sweet black type used in frying *kway teow*)
20 cloves garlic, pounded fine

Boil bamboo shoots for 5 minutes and drain. When cool, cut into fine strips. Do the same with turnip.

Boil belly pork and prawns in 1 litre water. Remove prawns after 5 minutes. Peel and set aside. Boil pork for 10 minutes more and remove to cool. Dice fine.

Heat oil in a *kwali* and fry crushed garlic until brown. Add preserved soy beans and fry till fragrant. Add all ingredients and stock and let simmer for 2 hours over low heat.

Keep in refrigerator overnight and reheat the next day. Let filling simmer over low heat while you prepare other ingredients.

How to Serve Popiah
Ladle bamboo shoot filling into a large tureen and place at the centre of a round table. Place all other ingredients and relishes in small bowls all around this. For the benefit of those who have never sat down to a homemade Popiah meal, this is the way to do it.

Take one piece of *popiah* skin. Cut another into two and place the half skin in the centre of the whole one. Place a piece of lettuce leaf (about 5 cm long) near the edge of the skins.

Now come the relishes. Spread 1 teaspoon chilli and 1 teaspoon sweet sauce on lettuce leaf. Add a little pounded garlic on top of this.

Spread 1 tablespoon beansprouts over relishes and spoon 2 tablespoons bamboo

shoot filling on this. Make sure there is not too much liquid or your *popiah* skin will get too moist and burst. Spread filling into an elongated shape about 8 cm long and garnish with a bit of each of the remaining ingredients.

Popiah Goreng
Make Popiah as usual but use two pieces of *popiah* skin to firmly wrap the rolls. Deep-fry in oil for 3 minutes until light brown

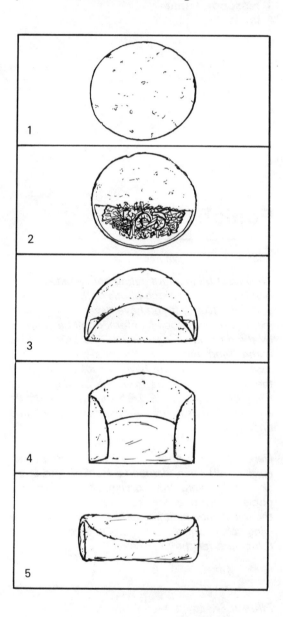

OPPOSITE: Sambal Serondeng (recipe p. 108).

PAGE 114: Clockwise from top, Sambal Babi (recipe p. 110), Pork Skin and Cucumber Sambal (recipe p. 111) and *chin char loke* (p. 86).

PAGE 115: Mee Siam (recipe p. 120).

Oodles of Noodles

That noodles—any kind as long as they were long—signified longevity was enough reason for the Straitsborn cooks to prepare them often. But noodles were elevated into a class of their own during birthdays and wedding ceremonies. Fried, stewed, made with rich stock or in sambal, noodles were a far cry from the pre-packed instant *mee* of today. But I do not decry packaged food and have had occasion to eat them when there was no time to do even the simplest cooking.

I remember my mother's favourite noodle dish — Laksa — whenever she had her cronies over to play a game of cards called *cherki*. Not going out to work and with no other form of entertainment, Nonya ladies of old turned to such gambling sessions when gossiping, not the game at hand, was the order of the day. But everything played a secondary role to the food. The reason for cooking noodles was it could be done beforehand and everyone was free to sit for hours at the square table dealing cards and eating while playing.

If they did take a break for lunch or dinner, it was only to help themselves from the plethora of cooked ingredients that went into Laksa. Plump prawns, cooked and sliced, finely shredded cucumber, fish cakes, shredded omelette and the all-important *laksa* leaves would be laid ready. The gravy would be fuming over a charcoal stove in the kitchen and it was usually my job to keep the gravy boat replenished by running to and from the kitchen.

Sometimes she would cook Mee Siam, which was less tiring for me, and at other times the salty-savoury Nonya Mee. Whatever it was she cooked, there was always plenty left over for dinner and even breakfast the next day. And along with every noodle dish was the ever-present *sambal belacan*, always freshly made and tangy with shredded *limau purut* leaves.

Mee Sua with Kidney and Liver Soup

(Illustrated opposite)

Cooking time: 5 minutes

1 pair kidneys
150 g pig's liver
10 shallots, sliced
3 tablespoons oil
3 cloves garlic, crushed
50 g minced pork

750 millilitres water
4 bundles fine rice vermicelli, sold in
  boxes (Hokkien: *mee sua*)
2 teaspoons fish sauce
1 teaspoon pepper
1 bunch coriander leaves, chopped

OPPOSITE: Mee Sua with Kidney and Liver Soup (recipe above). Background, Ingredients for Sweet Noodles with Hard-boiled Eggs (recipe p. 121).

To prepare kidneys, force each one (where the aperture is) under a tap and turn on the water. The kidney will swell a little and ammonia odour will be reduced. Cut into two and remove every trace of white fat. Cut into pieces and score criss-cross patterns on each. Slice liver into thin pieces.

Fry shallots in oil until brown and remove. In remaining oil, fry garlic and add minced pork when garlic is brown. Add water and bring to a boil. Add vermicelli, kidneys, liver and seasoning and simmer for 2 minutes and no more. Overcooked kidneys and liver will taste like cardboard. Garnish with fried shallots and coriander leaves.

Nonya Mee

(Illustrated on p. 19)

Cooking time: 25 minutes

200 g belly pork, in one piece with skin
    removed
2 litres water
250 g prawns
5 tablespoons oil
6 cloves garlic, crushed fine
3 tablespoons preserved soy beans
    (Hokkien: *taucheo*), mashed
250 g fresh yellow noodles (Hokkien: *mee*)
100 g beansprouts, tailed
2 teaspoons salt
1 teaspoon monosodium glutamate

Ingredients for Garnish
10 shallots, sliced fine
1 cucumber
2 eggs for omelette
1 bunch coriander leaves, chopped
    (optional)
2 red chillies, sliced (optional)

Boil belly pork in one piece in 2 litres water for 10 minutes. Remove and set aside. Keep stock hot. Wash prawns and dry-fry in a separate pan until they turn pink. Put prawns in a wire sieve with handle and boil in stock for 3 minutes. Remove prawns and shell. Cut cooled pork into bite-sized pieces.

Heat oil in a *kwali* and fry shallots (one of the ingredients for garnishing) until brown. Remove and set aside.

In remaining oil fry crushed garlic until brown and set aside, leaving about 1 teaspoon garlic still in the *kwali*. Add mashed preserved soy beans to oil and fry for 2 minutes. Add pork and fry for 1 minute.

Pour in stock and bring to a boil. Add noodles and beansprouts to cook for 5 minutes, stirring with long-handled chopsticks and a ladle. You can either add the shelled prawns to noodles at this stage or use as garnish. Add seasoning. Add more water if necessary but adjust seasoning.

Garnishes
Skin cucumber and with a sharp knife or vegetable slicer, cut into paper-thin pieces and shred as fine as possible. Beat eggs and make an omelette for shredding.

Garnish noodles with egg, fried shallots and cucumber. Fresh coriander and cut red chillies can be added if you like. Serve with *sambal belacan*.

Fried Bee Hoon with Cabbage

Cooking time: 10 minutes

1 packet coarse rice vermicelli (Hokkien: *bee hoon*)
1 litre boiling hot water
4 dried soybean pieces (Hokkien: *tee taukee*, Cantonese: *tim chok*)
6 tablespoons oil
4 tablespoons dried prawns, soaked in hot water
¼ cabbage, sliced fine
2 teaspoons salt

Soak vermicelli in boiling water for 5 minutes. Drain.

Cut dried soybean lengthwise into pieces 1 cm wide. Fry in hot oil until they curl and become brown and crisp. Cool and keep in an airtight bottle for the time being.

In remaining oil fry dried prawns for 3 minutes and add cabbage and vermicelli and continue frying for about 5 minutes. Add salt and water and stir until vermicelli is cooked. Serve garnished with fried soybean pieces.

Mee Goreng Terry

Cooking time: 25 minutes

1 potato
4 tablespoons oil
4 tablespoons water
1 large onion, sliced
100 g beansprouts
300 g fresh yellow noodles (Hokkien: *mee*)
3 eggs
100 g shrimps, shelled
3 tomatoes, quartered
1 teaspoon salt
2 tablespoons tomato ketchup
3 green chillies, sliced coarsely
1 cucumber, sliced

Rempah
5 dried chillies
1 large onion
2 cloves garlic

Boil potato for 10 minutes. Skin and cut into small cubes.

Heat 2 tablespoons oil and fry *rempah* for 5 minutes. Add water and simmer for 3 minutes. Remove from pan.

Put remaining oil into pan. Fry onion, beansprouts and noodles well for 3 minutes and, making a well in centre, break eggs in one by one. Put shrimps, potato, tomatoes, salt and tomato ketchup in and stir well. Just before dishing up, add green chillies and *rempah*. Serve with sliced cucumber.

Mee Siam

(Illustrated on p. 115)

Cooking time: 25 minutes

Mee Siam and Sambal
water for scalding vermicelli
1 packet coarse rice vermicelli (Hokkien: *bee hoon*)
250 g beansprouts
100 g Chinese chives (Hokkien: *koo chye*)
500 g small prawns
3 tablespoons oil
4 firm soybean cakes (Hokkien: *taukwa*)
5 tablespoons oil
1 large onion, sliced
250 millilitres water ⎱ *mixed*
2 tablespoons tamarind powder ⎰
4 hardboiled eggs, sliced

Rempah
5 tablespoons dried prawns (pounded separately)
5 large onions
4 cloves garlic
6 candlenuts
20 dried chillies
3 tablespoons *belacan* powder
1 teaspoon sugar ⎱ *added after*
1 teaspoon salt ⎰ *frying rempah*

Gravy
2 litres water
4 tablespoons tamarind powder ⎱ *mixed*
3 tablespoons fried *rempah* (see method)
2 tablespoons preserved soy beans (Hokkien: *taucheo*), mashed a little
2 teaspoons sugar
¼ coconut, grated
150 millilitres water

Basic Preparation of Ingredients
Boil a large kettle of water and scald vermicelli for 10 minutes, longer if necessary to soften until strands are pliable and soft to the touch.

Wash and tail beansprouts. Cut chives into 4 cm lengths. Wash and drain. Wash and peel prawns.

Heat 3 tablespoons oil and fry firm soybean cakes until brown. Cut into pieces 1 × 2 × ½ cm.

Sambal
Heat 5 tablespoons oil and fry pounded dried prawns for 3 minutes. Add all other *rempah* ingredients except sugar and salt and fry until oil seeps out again. Add sugar and salt and stir once. Remove about half the amount of *rempah* and put aside.

In remaining *rempah*, add sliced onion and fry for 2 minutes. Add prawns and tamarind liquid and simmer for five minutes. Remove and set aside.

How to Fry Vermicelli
Putting all but 3 tablespoons of the reserved *rempah* in a *kwali*, fry vermicelli and beansprouts for 8–10 minutes, stirring all the time until cooked. Moisten occasionally with tamarind liquid from the gravy allowance if vermicelli gets dry during frying. Add about 3 tablespoons of fried soybean pieces and half the chives to this fried vermicelli. Dish up and arrange on a large plate with sliced hardboiled eggs, remaining chives and remaining soybean pieces for garnish.

Gravy
Bring tamarind liquid to a boil. Put all ingredients in. Adjust seasoning to suit your taste.

Serve Mee Siam with sambal prawns and as much gravy as each person wants from a gravy boat.

Sweet Noodles with Hardboiled Eggs

(Illustrated on p. 116)

Cooking time: 15 minutes

If ever there was a symbolic dish, this is it. Only at birthdays would this be served with much exhortation to finish every drop if one was to grow a year older. The noodles signified longevity, the sugar a sweet life. I'm not too sure what the eggs signified except that they would be coloured red. Red eggs are normally given away at a baby's first birthday which comes a month—not a year—after its birth. I used to hate this dish until I was much older when I found it very nice.

1.5 litres water
150 g sugar
1 small lump rock sugar
300 g dry flat noodles, usually sold lightly floured (Hokkien: *mee teow*)
4 hardboiled eggs, dipped into red food colouring to streak it a little

Boil water with both types of sugar until completely dissolved and strain. Scald noodles lightly to remove flour and drain under tap quickly. To serve, put one egg in a bowl and a handful of noodles topped with the syrup.

Rice and All Things Nice

Though Nonyas turned their noses down at fried rice (they considered it beneath their skills to fry up such an easy thing), when my mother did make her version, it was like nothing I had eaten before. When I was a child, eating out was something that happened only on the rare occasion and then it was invariably at places like the Satay Club or the swimming club, of which my father was a member. Sometimes there would be Yang Chow fried rice which my mother would totally ignore. Perhaps other Straits Chinese did not react this way but, in my family, fried rice, if to be served at all, demanded more than the token two stirs and an egg. Twenty years later, I must admit that fried rice is one of the most handy one-dish meals to cook when you hardly have time to eat and are just so fed up with hawker food. Writing a food column has enabled me to experiment with many types of fried rice but the best still remains *nasi goreng*, Nonya style. Spices of the Orient has a bottled fried rice seasoning that is almost like the *nasi goreng sambal* my mother used to make.

Fried Rice Orient

(Illustrated on p. 133)

Cooking time: 5 minutes

4 tablespoons oil
2 eggs, beaten
1 large onion, sliced
3 tablespoons pounded dried prawns
150 g cooked shrimps
300 g cold cooked rice
2 tablespoons fried rice seasoning (a Spices of the Orient product)
2 teaspoons salt
shredded lettuce

Heat oil and fry beaten egg till cooked. Shred with ladle and push aside. Fry sliced onion till soft. Lift out both ingredients. In remaining oil, fry dried prawns till fragrant. Add all other ingredients except lettuce and fry well for 3 minutes. Serve garnished with lettuce shreds.

Nasi Ulam

Cooking time: 10 minutes

Undoubtedly the queen of all Nonya rice dishes, Nasi Ulam is rarely prepared today as it requires so many different fresh herbs. In this case, powdered substitutes just won't do but this recipe is a simplified one which uses about half the usual number of herbs which are still easily available. It is always served cold.

2 *selar* (yellowstripe trevally)
6 tablespoons oil
4 shallots, sliced very fine
4 cloves garlic, sliced very fine
1 teaspoon salt
1 teaspoon monosodium glutamate
  (optional)
400 g cold cooked rice

Ingredients to be Sliced Very Fine
3 long beans
1 stalk lemon grass
3 *daun limau purut*
1 *daun kemangi/selaseh* (basil leaf)
6 *daun kesom* (polygonum)
1 turmeric leaf

Cucumber and Belacan Sambal
1 cucumber
2 tablespoons *sambal belacan* (p. 86)
2 teaspoons sugar
juice of 1 lime

Traditionally, Nasi Ulam calls for the fish to be baked or grilled and then shredded, but frying will do just as well to simplify matters. In the remaining oil (after frying fish), fry shallots and garlic until they are crisp. The other ingredients must be sliced very fine to make Nasi Ulam what it is. Mix all, including salt and monosodium glutamate, with rice and shredded fish and serve with cucumber and *belacan sambal* (see below).

Cucumber and Belacan Sambal
Cube cucumber very fine and mix with *sambal belacan*, sugar and lime juice.

Fried Rice Shanghai Style

Cooking time: 5 minutes

5 tablespoons oil
1 Chinese sausage (Cantonese:
  lap cheong)
1 large onion, sliced
2 eggs
300 g cold cooked rice
150 g cooked shrimps
1 slice cooked ham, cut into
  small pieces
2 teaspoons salt
1 teaspoon monosodium glutamate

Heat oil and fry *lap cheong* till brown. Cool and slice diagonally. In remaining oil fry sliced onion till soft. Push aside and break eggs in to fry. Break up yolk and stir well to break into shreds. Add rice and stir constantly for 3 minutes. Add shrimps, ham and seasoning and stir for a few minutes more till well mixed.

Nasi Biryani with Chicken

Cooking time: 40 minutes

This is not strictly a Nonya dish but is nevertheless cooked often as a spicy change. I learnt this not too long ago from a former Indian colleague.

Rice
3 or 4 saffron strands
5 tablespoons water
500 g Basmati (long-grain) rice
2 tablespoons ghee
6 shallots, sliced
100 millilitres evaporated milk
1 litre water ⎫ mixed
1 teaspoon salt ⎭
1 packet raisins

Biryani Chicken
½ coconut, grated
500 millilitres water
100 millilitres evaporated milk
4 tablespoons ground almonds
juice of 1 lime
3 tablespoons ghee
2 tablespoons ground ginger
5 cm stick cinnamon
6 cardamoms
3 green chillies, split
   lengthwise
1 bunch coriander leaves, chopped
1 chicken, about 1½ kg, cut into
   6 joints
2 teaspoons salt

Rempah
5 cloves garlic
1 tablespoon ground coriander
1 teaspoon ground turmeric
1 teaspoon ground cummin
1 teaspoon ground aniseed
1 teaspoon chilli powder
1 teaspoon pepper

Soak saffron strands in 5 tablespoons water until liquid is golden yellow. Wash Basmati rice and drain. Heat pan with ghee and fry sliced shallots until brown. Add rice and fry quickly, making sure rice doesn't stick to pan. Add milk mixed with water and salt and transfer to a pot or rice cooker to finish cooking.

When rice is almost dry, with still a little moisture on top, sprinkle saffron water (remove saffron strands first) on top of rice and stir it to get a combination of yellow and white grains. Cover and continue cooking until dry. Add raisins in the last few minutes and leave to plump up in hot rice.

Squeeze coconut with water for coconut milk. Mix coconut milk and evaporated milk and add ground almonds. Squeeze lime juice over mixture and leave for a few minutes to curdle.

Heat ghee and fry ground ginger for 1 minute. Add *rempah*, cinnamon, cardamoms, green chillies and coriander leaves and fry for a further 2 minutes. Add chicken joints and fry until all the pieces are well coated with *rempah*. Add prepared liquid and salt and simmer for 25 minutes. Gravy should be reduced by about half.

Pile chicken joints onto Biryani rice and cover to let steep.

Nasi Goreng Nya Bulat

Cooking time: 15 minutes

In case you're wondering, Nya Bulat was my mother's nickname, by which she was well-known among our neighbours for her wonderful cooking skills. She often made this fried rice (the only one she would cook) and there wouldn't be a single grain left after a meal.

4 chillies
1 tablespoon *belacan*, **toasted**
4 tablespoons oil
2 eggs, beaten
**200 g dried prawns, soaked in
  hot water till soft, then
  pounded fine**
600 g cold cooked rice
150 g shrimps, shelled
1 teaspoon salt
1 teaspoon fish sauce
1 teaspoon monosodium glutamate

Pound chillies with toasted *belacan* for *sambal belacan*.

Heat oil and fry beaten eggs into an omelette. Remove and cool. In remaining oil, fry dried prawns until fragrant. Add cold rice and stir well for 5 minutes. Add shrimps and continue to stir for a few minutes.

Make a well in the centre of the pan and put in *sambal belacan* to cook for a few seconds. Mix well with rice and add seasoning.

To serve, cut omelette into fine strips and garnish rice.

Soups of the Nonyas

No mere liquid sustenance, Nonya soups, few though there are, never fail to win *aficionados* after their first tentative sip. I had an Australian friend once who spent minutes describing to me this delicious, loose stew she had at her Nonya friend's house during Chinese New Year. 'It had pork and duck and a soft vegetable and tasted subtly of brandy,' she enthused. Of course she was talking about the Nonya soup of soups— Itek Tim or duck and salted vegetable soup. Then there are the spicy soups like Titiek which is a veritable meal in itself and clear ones made from chicken with a hint of ginger and pepper. Dark soups based on tamarind liquid are usually brimming with seafood like prawns and cuttlefish but some of these are really considered curries rather than soup. Whatever, Nonya soups are quite different from the consommés of the Western world which are meant to whet the appetite for other things to come. Rich and oily or tart and light, each Nonya soup is a small masterpiece of blends with each family adding its own little touches that make it subtly different from any other.

Stuffed Cuttlefish Soup

Cooking time: 8 minutes

6 medium-sized cuttlefish or squid
250 g minced pork
150 g prawns, shelled and minced
1 teaspoon cornflour
1 teaspoon salt } *mixed*
2 tablespoons water
2 tablespoons oil
2 cloves garlic, crushed
800 millilitres water
1 teaspoon pepper
2 teaspoons fish sauce
1 stalk Chinese parsley, chopped

Wash cuttlefish, removing tentacles and ink sac. Discard ink sac. Mix minced pork and prawns with cornflour mixture and stuff each cuttlefish with it. Do not stuff too full as cuttlefish shrinks when cooked, forcing mixture out. Stuff about two-thirds full and fix tentacles back, securing with a toothpick.

Heat oil and fry garlic till brown. Add water and bring to a boil. Transfer to a soup pot and add stuffed cuttlefish. Simmer for 5 minutes and add seasoning. Serve garnished with Chinese parsley.

Chicken and Macaroni Soup

Cooking time: 30 minutes

250 g macaroni elbows or shells
2 chicken breasts
2 litres water
1 chicken bouillon cube
1 teaspoon fish sauce
6 shallots, sliced
6 tablespoons oil
2 slices day-old bread, cut into cubes
1 bunch coriander leaves, chopped
2 red chillies, sliced

Bring a large pot of water to a boil and put macaroni in to boil for 12 minutes. To test if macaroni is cooked, bite one piece. If it is soft but has a little 'give' it is done—as the Italians who invented this *pasta* called it—*al dente*. Overcooking will make it mushy and undercooking will yield hard macaroni. When macaroni is cooked, wash under tap so shells don't stick together.

Simmer chicken breasts for 15 minutes in 2 litres water and add chicken bouillon cube and fish sauce. Remove chicken and dice.

Fry shallots in oil till brown. Remove. In remaining oil, fry cubed bread into croutons.

Assemble ingredients in individual bowls: as much macaroni as desired with 2 tablespoons chicken meat, fried shallots and croutons. Top up with hot soup and garnish with coriander leaves or cut red chillies.

Cucumber and Egg Drop Soup

Cooking time: 8 minutes

5 shallots, sliced
2 tablespoons oil
1 cucumber
700 millilitres water
100 g small prawns or 100 g lean pork
2 teaspoons fish sauce
pinch of monosodium glutamate
1 egg, lightly beaten

Fry shallots in oil till brown. Leave aside.

Skin cucumber and remove soft centre. Cut into four lengthwise and cut each length diagonally into 1 cm wide pieces.

Bring water to a boil and put all ingredients in except egg. Lower heat and, while simmering, dribble egg in with a swirling motion so you have it in shreds.

Pong Tauhu Soup

Cooking time: 20 minutes

Meatballs
400 g minced pork
500 g small prawns, shelled and minced
  (reserve shells for stock)
250 g soft soybean cake
  (Hokkien: *tauhu*)
1 teaspoon salt
1 teaspoon cornflour mixed with 2
  tablespoons water
1 egg, lightly beaten
1 tablespoon fried, crushed garlic
1 teaspoon pepper
½ teaspoon monosodium glutamate

Soup
prawn shells (reserved from above)
2.5 litres water
200 g streaky pork
3 tablespoons lard
2 cloves garlic, pounded
1 tablespoon preserved soy beans
  (Hokkien: *taucheo*), mashed
400 g tinned bamboo shoots, sliced into
  fine strips
1 stalk spring onion, chopped
1 teaspoon salt

Mix together all meatball ingredients and knead well to break up soft soybean cake. Mould into small balls the size of marbles. Test for seasoning by boiling one and tasting it. Adjust seasoning to taste.

Fry reserved prawn shells in a dry pan till pink, then pound. Bring water to a boil and put pounded shells in to simmer for stock. Strain stock.

Bring stock to a boil again and add streaky pork to boil for 15 minutes. Remove to cool and shred.

Heat lard and fry pounded garlic and preserved soy beans until fragrant. Ladle into stock and add bamboo shoots, pork, meatballs and spring onion. Season. When soup boils and meatballs float to the top, they are done. The soup should be tinged a delicate pink.

Radish and Dried Cuttlefish Soup

Cooking time: 25 minutes

1 radish
1 dried cuttlefish
900 millilitres water
50 g belly pork, sliced fine
1 teaspoon salt or 3 teaspoons fish sauce
pinch of monosodium glutamate
2 cloves garlic, chopped and fried in oil
  till brown

Scrape radish and cut diagonally into rounds about 1 cm thick. Soak dried cuttlefish in hot water for 10 minutes and, using kitchen scissors, cut into strips 2 cm wide and 3 cm long.

Bring water to a boil and put cuttlefish in to boil for 15 minutes. Add radish, pork and seasoning. Simmer for 10 minutes more and serve with fried garlic.

Bee Tai Mak Soup

Cooking time: 15 minutes

Bee Tai Mak, a rice flour noodle shaped like tear drops and sold by kway teow *hawkers, is a favourite supper dish of the Nonyas. It also appears at wedding lunches and the bride, not supposed to eat heartily during the dinner reception, would sip at a small bowl to sustain her during the long ceremony. Nonya Bee Tai Mak soup, with the addition of liver, is a more refined version of that sold by hawkers.*

**200 g *bee tai mak*, fresh from market
    stalls
2 tablespoons lard
1 clove garlic, crushed
100 g minced pork, mixed with 1 teaspoon
    cornflour and 1 tablespoon water
600 millilitres water
100 g prawns, shelled
100 g liver, sliced very thin
100 g beansprouts, tailed
2 teaspoons fish sauce
1 teaspoon pepper
pinch of monosodium glutamate
1 stalk spring onion, chopped**

Scald *bee tai mak* in boiling water for 1 minute and run under cold tap quickly to prevent sticking.

Heat lard and fry garlic until brown. Add minced pork and stir well to prevent lumps forming. Add water and bring to a boil. Add prawns, liver and beansprouts. Simmer for 1 minute and add fish sauce, pepper and monosodium glutamate.

Pour soup over *bee tai mak* in individual bowls and serve garnished with spring onion.

Tauhu Titiek

(Illustrated on p. 133)

Cooking time: 8 minutes

**4 tablespoons oil
100 g *kurau* (threadfin) saltfish bones,
    soaked in water for 5 minutes
200 g small prawns, shelled
750 millilitres water
1 teaspoon fish sauce
½ teaspoon pepper
1 large soft soybean cake (Hokkien:
    tauhu), cut into 6 pieces
pepper
1 bunch coriander leaves, chopped**

Rempah
**4 candlenuts
2 large onions
2 red chillies
1 tablespoon *belacan* powder**

Fry *rempah* in oil until fragrant. Put saltfish bones and prawns in to fry for 2 minutes and add water, fish sauce and pepper. Bring to a boil and add soft soybean cake to simmer for 3 more minutes. Serve with an extra dash of pepper and coriander leaves.

Chap Chye Soup

Cooking time: 45 minutes

30 lily buds (Hokkien: *kim chiam*)
4 dried soybean pieces (Hokkien: *tee taukee*, Cantonese: *tim chok*)
3 tablespoons tree fungus (Hokkien: *bok jee*)
30 g transparent vermicelli (Hokkien: *tunghoon*)
6 Chinese mushrooms, stems removed
250 g small prawns
1 tablespoon oil
2 litres water
5 tablespoons oil
4 cloves garlic, pounded
2 tablespoons preserved soy beans (Hokkien: *taucheo*), mashed
300 g belly pork, cut into bite-sized strips
¼ cabbage, cut into large pieces
1 teaspoon salt

Soak lily buds, soybean pieces, fungus, vermicelli and mushrooms in water for 15 minutes.

Wash and shell prawns. Reserve shells. Fry prawn shells in a hot pan with a little oil, then pound. Add to 2 litres water and simmer for 10 minutes. Strain through sieve.

Drain dried ingredients. Remove hard tips of lily buds and tie into knots. Cut each soybean piece into 3.

Heat oil and fry garlic until brown. Add preserved soy beans and fry for 2 minutes. Add pork, cabbage and lily buds and fry for a further 3 minutes. Add remaining ingredients and fry for 2 minutes. Transfer everything to the large pot of stock, add salt and simmer for 30 minutes.

Hee Peow Soup

(Illustrated on p. 19)

Cooking time: 1 hour 25 minutes

The hee peow *referred to is dried fish bladder sold at most dry goods stalls in markets. Do not confuse this with dried pork skin as both look rather similar. Ask for it by name.*

2 pieces *hee peow*
150 g pork, minced
150 g prawns, shelled and minced
1 teaspoon salt
1 kg pork ribs or bones
3 litres water
20 fishballs
½ cabbage, cut into large pieces
2 teaspoons salt
1 teaspoon pepper
5 cloves garlic, crushed
4 tablespoons oil
1 sprig coriander leaves, chopped

Soak *hee peow* in water for 5 minutes, then cut into large pieces. Mix minced pork, prawns and 1 teaspoon salt and mould into small balls.

Put pork ribs or bones to boil with water and let simmer for an hour. Steam fishballs and minced pork and prawn balls for 5 minutes.

Remove bones from stock and skim off fatty froth from surface. Add all other ingredients except garlic, oil and coriander leaves and simmer for 15 minutes.

For garnish, fry crushed garlic in oil until brown and sprinkle on soup just before serving. Coriander leaves may also be added.

Itek Tim
(Kiam Chye Soup with Duck)

(Illustrated on p. 18)

Cooking time: 1 hour

1 whole duck, cut into 6–8 pieces
1 tablespoon brandy
500 g salted vegetable (Hokkien: *kiam chye*), with more stalk than leaves
3 litres water (2 if a pressure cooker is used)
200 g foreleg of pork with fat (Hokkien: *tui bak*), or a small pig's trotter, cut into pieces
2 sour plums (Hokkien: *sng boey*)
1 piece tamarind skin
1 teaspoon monosodium glutamate
2 tomatoes
3 green chillies
1 tablespoon brandy (optional)

Rub duck pieces with brandy and leave aside for 10 minutes. If you want just a subtle hint of brandy, rinse the pieces with cold water before cooking. Soak *kiam chye* in several changes of water for 15 minutes.

Bring water to a boil and put duck, pork or pig's trotter, sour plums, tamarind skin and seasoning in to boil.

You would need to simmer for a good hour before putting in the rest of the ingredients if you are cooking on the range. Reduce liquid by 1 litre if you are using the pressure cooker. Pressure cook the meat for 20 minutes, then add vegetables and cook for 10–15 minutes. If range cooking, put both ingredients in at the same time. Add tomatoes in last 5 minutes of cooking.

To serve, break green chillies over soup and add brandy, if desired.

My Teochew, Hokkien and Cantonese Heritage

Growing up in an extended family was enriching enough. But the influence exerted by many non-family members in culinary styles was equally rich. My family had always had several family retainers but none was so remarkable as the one from the Fukien province of South China.

She had come from China some 50 years earlier, had brought my mother up and proceeded to spoil my sister and elder brother rotten. She was wet nurse, surrogate mother, disciplinarian, but best of all, she was a supercook of Hokkien dishes. Thus, though we were a typical Straitsborn family, the food we ate was often a mixture of ethnic Chinese and Nonya. This lady—we called her Hokkien Sim (Hokkien aunt) and never knew her real name till the day she died—was from sturdy peasant stock. She used to regale us with the story of why she had come from China. 'It was the best way not to have any more children by my husband,' was her explanation. She cooked the most mouth-watering, gut-filling dishes, using the simplest of ingredients, and was an expert at using up leftovers. Her penchant for emptying several half-finished dishes into one at the dinner table caused a few eyebrows to be raised whenever we had guests.

In later years, there were other baby *amahs* in the house, women who came and did the washing and ironing and were practically part of the household, and my sisters-in-law who were from the different dialect groups. They shared with the family their Hakka, Chiakwan (a district in Fukien province) and Teochew recipes.

And when I married my Cantonese wife, her mother, a true-blue Cantonese married to a Baba herself, taught me a great deal that I never knew before. Don't you believe all that stuff about mothers-in-law being battleaxes because mine is a gem and the mother I haven't had for so many years.

I learnt to cook such classic Cantonese dishes as yam cakes, stir-fried vegetables and claypot dishes of the most unctuous and oily-rich meats, fish and dried vegetables. Since my mother herself was a Teochew Nonya, she had also retained some traditional Teochew recipes. She still knew how to steam fish, innocent of any but the subtlest hint of ginger, how to make the most mouth-watering desserts from simple tapioca and bananas.

It was from this delightful mish-mash of culinary influences that I developed a love of food. Sundays were particularly glorious when everyone pitched in (to show off their skills really) and the lunch table would be creaking under such good things as Hokkien fried noodles, Nonya Nasi Goreng and Satay Babi, finished off with the sticky-sweet Teochew dessert of Oh Nee—a rich dessert made with yam and tons of sugar.

OPPOSITE: Fried Rice Orient (recipe p. 122). Top, Tauhu Titiek (recipe p. 129).

Terry's Chicken Stew
TEOCHEW

Cooking time: 20 minutes

1 chicken, about 1½ kg
2 tablespoons black soy sauce
4 potatoes
2 large onions
2 carrots
3 tablespoons oil
800 millilitres water
1 chicken bouillon cube
5 cloves
4 cm stick cinnamon
1 tablespoon cornflour
2 tablespoons water

Wash and cut chicken into 8 pieces, discarding head and claws. Marinate in soy sauce for half an hour. Cut potatoes into wedges. Quarter onions and slice carrots diagonally into 4 cm pieces.

Drain chicken, reserving marinade. Fry in hot oil until skin turns brown. Remove chicken from oil and fry potatoes, onions and carrots for 2 minutes. Remove these from oil and add water, chicken bouillon cube, cloves, cinnamon and chicken pieces, and bring to a boil. Simmer for 15 minutes and add potatoes, onions and carrots. Mix cornflour with 2 tablespoons water and add to stew. Simmer for another 5 minutes and serve with bread and butter.

Bak Kng
(Minced Pork Rolls)
HOKKIEN

(Illustrated opposite)

Cooking time: 5 minutes

500 g minced pork, mixed with
   3 tablespoons diced pork fat
200 g prawns, shelled and diced
6 water chestnuts, peeled and diced
3 cloves garlic, crushed
150 g crabmeat (fresh or frozen)
1 stalk spring onion, chopped
1 bunch coriander leaves, chopped
1 egg
2 teaspoons salt
1 teaspoon pepper
1 tablespoon cornflour
4 tablespoons water
2 sheets soybean skin (brown, round
   sheets, *tau fu pei* in Cantonese)
oil for deep-frying

PAGE 134: Left to right, Saltfish Rice in Clay Pot (recipe p. 140) and Sweetcorn and Chicken Soup (recipe p. 141).

PAGE 135: Lo Kai Yik (recipe p. 142).

OPPOSITE: Bak Kng (recipe above).

Mix all except last two ingredients together well. Test for seasoning by boiling a small amount, rolled into a ball, in some water. Adjust seasoning if necessary.

Spread whole soybean skin on the table and put 2 tablespoons of mixture on skin at one end. Roll twice over and cut off excess. Moisten long edge with water to seal and fold both ends under to form a firm spring roll. Continue doing this until skin or mixture is used up.

Deep-fry in hot oil for 4 or 5 minutes and serve, cut into diagonal pieces. Eat with commercial chilli sauce or make your own dip. An easy, fast one is an equal mixture of oyster sauce and garlic chilli sauce (p. 141).

Fried Hokkien Mee

Cooking time: 25 minutes

200 g pork lard, cubed
250 g belly pork
150 g prawns
150 g cuttlefish
1 litre water for stock
5 cloves garlic, crushed
3 eggs
500 g fresh yellow noodles
 (Hokkien: *mee*)
150 g coarse rice vermicelli
 (Hokkien: *bee hoon*), soaked
 in hot water for 10 minutes
150 g beansprouts, tailed
2 tablespoons fish sauce
100 g Chinese chives
 (Hokkien: *koo chye*),
 cut into 3 cm lengths

Fry lard until crisp. Set aside. It should have yielded about 4 tablespoons oil. Wash pork, prawns and cuttlefish and boil in 1 litre water. Lift out prawns and cuttlefish after 2 minutes and continue boiling pork for 5 more minutes. Lift out pork and reserve stock. Cut pork into strips. Shell prawns and slice each into two lengthwise. Cut cuttlefish into rings, removing ink sacs.

In the hot oil obtained in the first step, fry crushed garlic until brown and push to one side. Crack eggs in and stir to break up yolk. Add noodles, vermicelli and beansprouts and pour about 100 millilitres stock in. Stir for 1 minute, cover and leave to cook for 2 minutes.

Remove cover and stir well for 3 or 4 minutes. Add more stock and continue frying for 5 minutes. Add pork, prawns and cuttlefish and stir until mixture is cooked, adding more stock to get a wet consistency. Add fish sauce and chives and stir once. Serve with cut red chillies or *sambal belacan* with lime juice.

Taukwa Goreng Chye Poh

HOKKIEN

Cooking time: 5 minutes

1 large piece preserved
 radish (Hokkien: *chye poh*)
2 firm soybean cakes
 (Hokkien: *taukwa*)
3 cloves garlic
5 tablespoons oil
2 tablespoons sugar
4 tablespoons water

Soak preserved radish in water for 10 minutes and squeeze out all moisture. Cut into thin strips the size of potato chips. Cut soybean cakes into 2 x 2 x 1 cm pieces. Crush garlic.

Heat oil and fry soybean cake pieces till brown. Remove from pan and fry crushed garlic till brown. Add preserved radish and fry until fragrant. Add sugar, stirring to prevent caramel forming. Sprinkle a few drops of water while frying and add soybean cake pieces when mixture turns brown. Add water and simmer for 2 minutes.

Hokkien Mee Soup

Cooking time: 1 hour

Ingredients for stock
6 litres water
3 pork stock bones (ask butcher
   for shoulder blade bones)
1 pig's tail
500 g pork ribs
1 lump rock sugar, the size
   of a large walnut
2 tablespoons black soy sauce
2 tablespoons fish sauce
1 teaspoon monosodium glutamate

Other Ingredients
250 g pork fillet
500 g large prawns
4 tablespoons oil
250 g pork lard, diced
3 fish cakes
20 shallots, sliced
800 g fresh yellow noodles
   (Hokkien: *mee*)
200 g beansprouts, tailed
200 g water convolvulus, cut
   into small stalks
5 red chillies, sliced
2 bunches coriander leaves
   chopped
2 stalks spring onions, chopped

Bring 6 litres water to a boil. Put in stock bones, pig's tail cut into 4 cm chunks, pork ribs, rock sugar, soy sauce, fish sauce and monosodium glutamate to simmer for 40 minutes. Test for seasoning and adjust by adding salt or fish sauce. Strain stock.

Boil pork fillet (for 5 minutes) and prawns (for 2 minutes) in stock. Remove pork and prawns and strain stock once again. Slice pork fine. Shell and slice each prawn into two lengthwise.

Heat 4 tablespoons oil and fry lard till crisp. Remove lard crisps to a dish and use the remaining oil to fry, separately, fish cakes (for 3 minutes) and shallots (till crisp). Slice fish cakes into thin pieces.

Boil a large pot of water and let each diner scald as much noodles, beansprouts and water convolvulus as he wants for 1 minute. Put in individual bowls and top with sliced pork, pig's tail, prawns, fish cakes, lard crisps, shallots, chillies and green garnishes. Top with soup.

Chicken, Mushroom and Quail's Egg Soup
CANTONESE

Cooking time: 30 minutes

1.5 litres water
2 chicken breasts, cubed
6 Chinese mushrooms, stalks
   removed and soaked in water
   for 5 minutes
10 quail's eggs, hardboiled
1 teaspoon salt
1 teaspoon fish sauce
½ teaspoon monosodium
   glutamate
1 teaspoon pepper

Bring water to a boil. Add chicken and mushrooms and simmer for 25 minutes. Add boiled quail's eggs and seasoning and simmer for 3 minutes.

The traditional method for this clear soup is slow cooking in a double boiler. The Cantonese swear this *tun* method produces much more nutrition in any dish but I cannot see the logic in it. Of course, during more languid times, people had more hours on their hands to man slow-cooking dishes but it is hardly possible today.

Hum Yu Fun
(Saltfish Rice in Clay Pot)
CANTONESE

(Illustrated on p. 134)

Cooking time: 25 minutes

150 g *kurau* (threadfin) saltfish
2 tablespoons lard
100 g roast pork (Cantonese: *char siew*)
1 large knob ginger
300 g rice
600 millilitres water
2 tablespoons black soy sauce
2 tablespoons sesame oil
2 tablespoons chopped spring onion

Fry saltfish in lard until crispy and fragrant. Remove to cool and shred into coarse pieces. Dice roast pork and cut ginger into thick slices. Meanwhile, boil rice with water.

While rice is cooking, reheat oil and fry ginger in it for 1 minute. Add roast pork, soy sauce and shredded saltfish and stir once. Ladle this mixture into rice, which should be almost dry by this time, and stir well. Taste for seasoning and adjust with more soy sauce or salt as necessary. Just before serving, stir in sesame oil and spring onion.

For Claypot Service
Heat a claypot (the type with a handle traditionally used for simmering herbs) for 10 minutes and transfer cooked rice into this. Let it steep for 10 minutes for the rice to absorb the smoky taste that you get cooking with this utensil. You can't cook rice properly in a clay pot over a gas stove. If you have a charcoal oven, do the whole cooking process in the clay pot for an even better flavour.

Winter Melon Soup with Chicken
CANTONESE

Cooking time: 8 minutes

250 g winter melon
(about half a medium-sized melon)
1 chicken breast
150 g small prawns
800 millilitres water
1 teaspoon salt
1 teaspoon fish sauce

Skin winter melon and remove seeds and soft pith. Cut into 5 x 3 x 1 cm pieces. Cut chicken breast into small cubes and shell prawns.

Bring water to a boil and cook chicken for 2 minutes. Add melon and prawns and simmer for 5 minutes. Add seasoning and serve hot as a clear soup appetiser.

See Yeow Kai
(Chicken in Soy Sauce)
CANTONESE

Cooking time: 40 minutes

2 tablespoons sugar
1 large knob galingale
1 chicken, about 1½ kg
1.5 litres water
4 tablespoons thick black
   soy sauce
2 teaspoons salt
2 teaspoons sugar

Garlic Chilli Sauce
3 red chillies
2 cloves garlic
pinch of salt
2 tablespoons vinegar
1 teaspoon sugar

Heat a non-stick pan and put sugar in to caramelize. When it turns brown and bubbles, put in galingale. Put whole chicken in and turn all around to coat with caramel. Add a little of the water if caramel is inadequate to cover chicken. Doing this singes the chicken skin and gives it a glaze.

Add soy sauce and turn chicken to coat further, then pour in all the water. Add salt and sugar and simmer for about 40 minutes if uncovered, or 30 minutes if your pan has a tight lid. Turn occasionally so chicken is evenly cooked. Lift to cool before carving. Serve with garlic chilli sauce (below) and cucumber.

Garlic Chilli Sauce
Pound chillies and garlic together with salt. Add vinegar and sugar.

Suk Mai Yung Gai Tong
(Sweetcorn and Chicken Soup)
CANTONESE

(Illustrated on p. 134)

Cooking time: 15 minutes

1 chicken breast, cubed
800 millilitres water
1 can creamed sweetcorn
1 teaspoon salt
1 teaspoon fish sauce
1 egg, lightly beaten
1 teaspoon pepper
1 tablespoon sesame oil
   (optional)

Either steam chicken breast or boil in 800 millilitres water for 10 minutes. Cube chicken when cool. Bring water or chicken stock to a boil once again and add chicken cubes. Add sweetcorn and allow to simmer for 5 minutes. Add salt and fish sauce and stir in lightly beaten egg. Serve with pepper sprinkled on top.

Some cooks thicken the soup with cornflour but cream sweetcorn and beaten egg give enough body to make this unnecessary. Stirring in 1 tablespoon warmed sesame oil gives the soup a special nutty flavour.

Lo Kai Yik
(Stewed Chicken Wings)
CANTONESE

(Illustrated on p. 135)

Cooking time: 40 minutes

Though this recipe is called by its Cantonese name and used to be a popular hawker food, sold by an itinerant who lustily shouted lo kai yik! *from the street, it has a plethora of ingredients. But the basis remains a rich, red gravy made with preserved soybean curd (*lam yee*) and* hoisin *sauce.*

200 g pork skin
4 cloves garlic
5 tablespoons oil
3 preserved soybean curd
     (Cantonese: *lam yee*)
3 tablespoons *hoisin* sauce
2 litres water
1 teaspoon sugar
10 chicken wings
150 g belly pork
200 g water convolvulus
4 chicken gizzards
2 chicken livers
10 dried soybean cakes
     (Hokkien: *tau pok*)

Chilli Dip
5 red chillies
2 cloves garlic
pinch of salt
1 teaspoon sugar
2 tablespoons vinegar

Boil pork skin for 25 minutes and cut into squares.

Crush garlic and saute in hot oil in a non-stick deep pot or *kwali*. When garlic is brown, break up soybean curd and fry for a few minutes. Add *hoisin* sauce and water and bring gravy to a boil. Add sugar.

Clean chicken wings but leave them whole. Cut pork into bite-sized pieces. Scald water convolvulus in hot water with a little oil in it and tie stalks into little bundles. Clean gizzards and livers and leave whole.

When gravy boils put in pork skin first. Simmer for 5 minutes and add all other ingredients, adding water convolvulus last. Simmer for 10 minutes and adjust seasoning with a little salt. This may not be necessary as soybean curd and *hoisin* sauce are already salty.

This is an excellent one-pot dish and may be eaten by itself or with bread or rice and a chilli dip, like the one below.

Chilli Dip
Pound chillies with garlic and a pinch of salt. When fine, add sugar and scoop up into side dishes. Add vinegar to make a thick sauce.

Braised Duck with Chestnuts, Dried Oysters and Liver Stuffing

CANTONESE

(Illustrated on p. 83)

Cooking time: 2 hours

There are three ways to prepare this dish: pressure cooking, which takes less than 40 minutes, double boiler braising which takes twice as long, and slow simmering, the method least demanding in the way of special utensils and the one I used for my recipe. You need a wide-mouthed non-stick pan or kwali, but any deep kwali will do as long as you tend constantly to the simmering duck.

15 chestnuts, soaked in hot water and skinned
15 dried oysters (Cantonese: ho see)
6 large dried Chinese mushrooms
150 g pig's liver
4 tablespoons oil
4 cloves garlic, crushed
3 tablespoons black soy sauce
3 tablespoons oyster sauce
1 teaspoon pepper
1 teaspoon salt
300 millilitres water
1 whole duck, about 1½ kg
3 tablespoons Chinese wine (Cantonese: fa chiew)
2 teaspoons five-spice powder
5 tablespoons black soy sauce
2 teaspoons sugar
4 tablespoons oil
3 litres water (1.5 litres if a pressure cooker or double boiler is used)

Soak chestnuts, oysters and mushrooms in hot water for half an hour. Boil liver in a little water and dice when cool.

Heat oil and fry garlic until brown. Add chestnuts, oysters and mushrooms (left whole, or cut into small pieces) and fry for 5 minutes. Add soy sauce, oyster sauce, pepper and salt. Stir well and add 300 millilitres water to make a thick stuffing. Remove from *kwali*, add liver and leave to cool.

Wash duck thoroughly, making sure the insides are clear of blood and traces of offal. Be careful not to split the cavity opening any further as you will need to sew it up after putting in stuffing. Pat dry and rub with wine, five-spice powder, soy sauce and sugar. Leave for 30 minutes.

In your clean non-stick pan or *kwali*, heat 4 tablespoons oil. Brown duck all over and remove to cool. When cool enough to handle, spoon prepared stuffing into cavity but not to the brim as expansion during cooking will force some out. Sew up slit with strong thread. You should have less than half of the stuffing left to be simmered outside with the duck.

Put duck into the *kwali*, add water and simmer for about 1½ hours, topping up with more water if necessary, and turning duck every 15 minutes. You need not worry about extra liquid diluting the taste as this is a strong flavoured dish. Between turns of the duck, cover with a tight lid so less evaporation takes place. (Alternatively, do not cover but top up with liquid that is a mixture of 4 parts water to 1 part soy sauce and 1 part oyster sauce.)

When cooked, the duck should have a beautiful brown glaze. How much longer you want to cook it depends on how tender you like your duck. Personally, I prefer the tenderness that still allows carving without the meat falling apart. Remove string and serve duck whole.

Yu Tou Mai Fun
(Fish Head and Bee Hoon Soup)
CANTONESE

Cooking time: 10–15 minutes

This is a typical Cantonese supper dish that uses a freshwater fish, sang yu *in Cantonese (garoupa or grouper), and coarse rice vermicelli. Although reference is made to a fish head, there is no reason why you should not use a whole fish if you cannot find a large enough head with sufficient meat.*

1 packet coarse rice vermicelli
  (Hokkien: *bee hoon*)
1 large *garoupa* (grouper) head
250 g mustard greens
  (Hokkien: *chye sim*)
3 tablespoons oil
2 large knobs ginger, bruised
2 litres water
2 teaspoons salt

Scald vermicelli in hot water till soft. Set aside. Wash *garoupa* head and cut into bite-sized pieces. Cut greens into short lengths.

Heat oil and fry bruised ginger. Add water and bring to a boil. Add all other ingredients and simmer for 5 minutes until fish head is cooked.

Note: You can also use *garoupa* fillet cut into slices.

Kuih-Kuih

The Nonya tradition of serving a whole array of mouth-watering cakes called *Kuih Kuih Cuci Mulut* reached its peak in the mid-fifties, in my family at least. But as the old people passed on, not only did the varieties decrease, the frequency with which these cakes were served fell as well. What was meant to be dessert after a meal slowly became relegated to festive occasions or when guests were in the house.

It was a matter of pride for Nonyas that their *kuih kuih* had to be the best in that *kampung* or at least along their street. I had one aunt who was most annoying. She would make several varieties of *kuih* and come to our house bearing them in *tingkats* (tiffin carriers) tied up in large batik squares. With great ceremony, she would open each one to reveal her Kuih Dada, Kuih Koo and Kuih Talam and ask for our opinion of each. But how could we when she would not let us eat them? 'No, no, you cannot eat. Just tell me the colour and smell are perfect,' was her admonition. Of course if we youngsters

dared be cheeky and say '*tak sedap*' (not nice to eat), we would earn a sharp tweak of our ears.

Though I was always annoyed at having to do the worst chores whenever my mother and aunts made their *kuih kuih* — beating eggs endlessly was hardly joy for an 11-year-old — I learnt much at their knees. Each aunt had her own speciality and beamed with pride when the others asked her to show her skill so they could learn more. Thus Jee Kim (second maternal aunt) glowed with pride when showing how she made her festive Kuih Koo so tasty we would not eat those made by anyone else. Not to be outdone, Sar Kor (third paternal aunt) rolled up her *kebaya* sleeves and steamed up the most heavenly Serikaya. And amid the fierce competition, the skills of cake-making reached such a level that they rubbed off almost everyone living in a Nonya household whether they were interested in cooking or not.

Steamed Tapioca with Grated Coconut and Sugar

Cooking time: 15 minutes

1 kg tapioca
1 coconut, grated without skin
200 g sugar
200 g tinned corn kernels

Peel tapioca and steam for 15 minutes. Allow to cool, remove central root and cut into cubes. Mix with coconut, sugar and corn kernels in the proportion 4 parts tapioca to 1 part each of the other ingredients.

Kuih Bangkit

Cooking time: 15 minutes
Baking time: 25 minutes

600 g sago flour
6 *pandan* (screwpine) leaves
1½ coconuts, grated
250 millilitres water
250 g sugar
4 *pandan* (screwpine) leaves
2 egg yolks
1 egg white
2 teaspoons baking powder
1 egg, beaten
sesame seeds

Dry-fry sago flour with 6 *pandan* leaves for 8 minutes, then cool. Squeeze coconut with water for milk. Put sugar, coconut milk and 4 *pandan* leaves to boil over low heat. Leave to cool completely.

Beat 2 egg yolks and 1 egg white till frothy and add to cooled mixture. Beat for 3 minutes more. Sift sago flour with baking powder into a bowl, make a well in the centre and pour in mixture. Stir slowly and knead into a soft dough. If you find the mixture too soft for rolling out, sift a little more sago flour in.

Roll dough out to about 1 cm thickness. Use *bangkit* cutters and cut out different shapes. Lift onto foil sheets dusted with a little sago flour. Brush each *bangkit* with beaten egg and sprinkle with sesame seeds.

Bake in a pre-heated oven (gas mark 5) for about 12 minutes or until light brown. When cool, store in airtight containers.

Tapioca Squares in Grated Coconut

Cooking time: 15 minutes

1 kg tapioca
1 teaspoon salt
300 g palm sugar
1 coconut, grated without skin
pinch of salt

Skin tapioca and cut into large chunks. Boil with 1 teaspoon salt for 10 minutes. Drain and leave to dry completely. Remove central root of tapioca and mash to form a dough-like mixture.

Melt sugar in small pot over a larger pot of hot water and add syrup to mashed tapioca, a little at a time. If mixture is too wet, stop adding syrup. Place mixture in a flat dish and press down with a spatula or the palm of your hand, gently. When cool, cut into squares or diamond shapes and roll in grated coconut with a pinch of salt added.

Pengat

Cooking time: 15 minutes

300 g yam
500 g sweet potatoes
6 ripe bananas (*pisang rajah*)
1½ coconuts, grated
2 litres water
500 g palm sugar
300 millilitres water
3 *pandan* (screwpine) leaves

Peel yam and cut into chunks. Peel sweet potatoes (choose the type with red meat for a more attractive presentation) and cut into similar-sized chunks. It does not matter how big or small as long as each is bite-sized. Cut each banana diagonally into bite-sized slices.

Squeeze coconut with 2 litres water for milk. Shave palm sugar into slivers and melt in 300 millilitres water in a pan over low heat. Wash *pandan* leaves thoroughly and tie into knots so they'll be easier to remove before serving. Put yam and sweet potatoes with coconut milk and palm syrup into a large pot and bring to a boil. Simmer for about 6 minutes, stirring to prevent sticking if you are not using a non-stick pot. Add bananas and simmer for another 5 minutes.

Another way of serving Pengat is to top each bowl with thick coconut milk for added relish. For this, you simply squeeze the grated coconut with 150 millilitres (of the 2 litres allowance) boiled, warm water and leave aside this thick milk. Squeeze the residue with remaining water to add to the pot.

Onde Onde
(Sweet Potato Balls)

Cooking time: 10 minutes

500 g sweet potatoes
7 *pandan* (screwpine) leaves
5 tablespoons plain flour
½ teaspoon salt
400 g palm sugar
1 coconut, grated without skin

Skin sweet pototoes and boil in plenty of water with 1 or 2 *pandan* leaves for 5 minutes or until cooked, depending on whether you boil them whole or in chunks. Mash while still warm.

Pound remaining *pandan* leaves and extract juice. Add *pandan* juice to sweet potato and mix well. Sift flour into this mixture and add salt.

Shave palm sugar into thin slivers. Take a lump of sweet potato mixture and flatten into a round about 5 cm in diameter. Put a few slivers of palm sugar in the centre and shape into a ball. Repeat until all dough is used up. Boil a large pot of water and drop balls into it. When they rise to the surface, they are done. Drain and roll in grated coconut while still warm.

Pulot Hitam

(Illustrated on p. 156)

Cooking time: 1½ hours

400 g *pulot hitam* (black glutinous rice)
4 litres water
250 g sugar
100 g palm sugar, cut into slivers
3 *pandan* (screwpine) leaves
2 tablespoons cornflour
3 tablespoons water
1 coconut, grated
175 millilitres warm boiled water
pinch of salt

Wash *pulot* thoroughly, picking out debris and foreign matter. Put to boil with half the amount of water allowed until liquid is reduced. Add remaining water and continue simmering for 40 minutes.

Add both kinds of sugar and *pandan* leaves and simmer for another 20 minutes over low heat. Test if *pulot* is ready by eating a few grains. If they are soft and plumped up and the liquid is thick, it is ready. Never add sugar to *pulot* at the start or the grains will never be cooked.

While *pulot* is simmering, dissolve cornflour in 3 tablespoons water and add to the pot. Bring to a boil once and remove from heat.

Squeeze coconut with 175 millilitres water for thick milk. Add a pinch of salt. Serve Pulot Hitam with 2 tablespoons thick coconut milk to each bowl.

Kuih Wajek

Cooking time: 45 minutes

Probably one of the least known Nonya desserts, this glutinous rice pudding has a rather alarming brown, oily appearance that can be off-putting. The little squares of Wajek, however, are delicious.

500 g glutinous rice
2 coconuts, grated
850 millilitres water
700 g palm sugar
4 or more *pandan* (screwpine) leaves cut into short pieces
250 g sugar

Soak rice in water overnight or for 6 hours. Squeeze coconut with 850 millilitres water for milk. Shave palm sugar into slivers.

Line a steaming pan with a layer of muslin. Place *pandan* pieces all over. Spread rice evenly in pan and steam for 35 minutes.

When cooked, mix with coconut milk, sugar (both types) and more *pandan* leaves if you like a stronger fragrance. Cook over low heat until mixture is thick and resistant to stirring. The colour should be a greasy brown.

Spread on a tray about 3 cm high and let cool. It will harden by then. Cut into diamond or square shapes and serve.

Kuih Keria

Cooking time: 30 minutes

When I was about 10, there used to be a Malay woman who bore a large cane basket on her head walking by our house every morning hawking her Kuih Keria. They were hot and delicious and made from sweet potatoes. My mother made friends with this woman and coaxed the recipe from her which, thankfully, I remember. In later years, eating Kuih Keria (doughnuts couldn't hold a candle to this woman's Keria) reminded me what a difference it made to substitute sweet potato with plain flour. This one is made with sweet potatoes.

600 g sweet potatoes
150 g glutinous rice flour
1 teaspoon salt
extra glutinous rice flour for dusting
   Kuih Keria
oil for deep-frying

Ingredients for Coating
250 g sugar
50 millilitres water
3 *pandan* (screwpine) leaves
50 g icing sugar for dusting Kuih Keria

Skin and boil sweet potatoes till soft, then mash and mix with sifted flour. Add salt and shape into rings the size of doughnuts. Dust each with a little flour and deep-fry till golden brown.

To make coating, boil sugar in water and add *pandan* leaves. Reduce heat and dip each Kuih Keria into syrup to coat thoroughly, then remove. When all are coated, put back into the pan and shake gently till almost dry. Dust with extra icing sugar and allow to cool.

Green Beans in Coconut Milk

(Illustrated on p. 156)

Cooking time: 1½ hours

1 coconut, grated
400 millilitres water
500 g green beans
2 litres water, more if required
300 g palm sugar, cut into slivers
sugar (add as desired)

Squeeze coconut with 400 millilitres water for milk. Wash green beans in several changes of water until all foreign matter has been removed. Put to boil with 2 litres water for 1 hour. If mixture seems too thick, add more water. When beans are cooked (they should be soft and broken up), add coconut milk and palm sugar and simmer for 10 minutes until sugar is dissolved. Taste for sweetness and adjust with white sugar.

Note: It takes quite a while to boil green beans so do not add coconut milk at the beginning or the long cooking process will turn coconut milk into oil.

Kuih Lapis

(Illustrated on p. 154)

Cooking time: 35 minutes

Undoubtedly the elite among Nonya cakes, some believe the Lapis came to Singapore via the Indonesian branch of the Nonyas. It was my wife, Dorothy, who experimented and perfected this recipe and in turn taught me how to make it, though my efforts are inferior to hers. I must confess the Lapis in the picture on p. 154 is the result of her skills.

10 egg yolks
180 g castor sugar
250 g butter
75 g plain flour, sifted
½ teaspoon cake spice mix (a Spices of the Orient product)
4 egg whites
2 tablespoons rum or brandy

Beat egg yolks and castor sugar until thick and creamy. In a separate bowl, cream butter till soft and add egg mixture a little at a time. Stir well till thoroughly mixed. Fold in flour and spice mix. Beat egg whites till stiff peaks form and fold into batter. Add rum or brandy and mix gently but well.

Grease and line a 14 × 20 cm tin. Pre-heat oven to gas mark 3 and bake the first layer (about 3 tablespoons batter) until light brown. After each layer is done, press gently all over with the base of a glass to remove any bubbles. You can also buy a special aluminium presser, which is simply a square piece of metal with a handle, from sundry shops.

Subsequent layers can be cooked under an electric grill on gas mark 4 or moderately high heat. Each layer should take about 4 minutes to brown. Watch it carefully or you're liable to end up with burnt Lapis. Repeat process until all the batter is used up.

For another version of Lapis, you can add chopped almonds and raisins. For this, divide the batter into two portions and add 50 g almonds to one and 50 g raisins to the other. Have alternate layers of almonds and raisins, preferably ending with an almond layer. This is because the raisins will look lumpy as a top layer whereas chopped almonds will give only a slightly grainy touch.

Sweet Potato and Ginger Dessert

Cooking time: 6 minutes

This was a favourite afternoon tea in my family and a very cheap way to feed a hungry family!

1½ kg sweet potatoes (preferably with red meat)
2 large knobs ginger
2 litres water
200 g sugar

Skin sweet potatoes and cut into large chunks. Skin ginger and bruise lightly.

Bring water to a boil and add sweet potatoes, ginger and sugar. Boil for 6 minutes until sweet potatoes are soft. The sweet potatoes are supposed to stem hunger (they do) and the ginger to dispel wind (it really does).

Kuih Pisang

(Illustrated on p. 153)

Cooking time: 15 minutes

6 ripe bananas (*pisang rajah*)
1½ coconuts, grated
800 millilitres water
1 packet, about 100 g, *tepung hoenkwe*
  (green bean flour)
250 g sugar
½ teaspoon salt

Steam bananas for 10 minutes and cut diagonally into 1 cm thick slices when cooled. Squeeze coconut with water for coconut milk.

Put flour in an enamel saucepan or non-stick pot and blend with half the coconut milk. Mix remaining coconut milk with sugar and salt and stir over low heat until completely dissolved. Remove from heat and pour flour mixture into this, stirring all the while. It must be done over very gentle heat or mixture will burn.

Remove mixture from heat and spread in a shallow dish or cake tin. Put banana slices, some inside the mixture and some on top, just buried a little so when you cut into slices, each slice will hold some banana. Chill before serving.

For an attractive presentation, put 2 tablespoons of the flour mixture with 2 or 3 slices of banana on banana leaves, previously washed and scalded and cut into 15 cm squares. Fold over banana leaves to form flat pancakes and chill.

Sago Pudding with Gula Melaka

Cooking time: 20 minutes

1 coconut, grated
200 millilitres water
350 g pearl sago
1 litre water
½ teaspoon salt
300 g palm sugar
1 coconut, grated
250 millilitres water
½ teaspoon salt

Squeeze coconut with 200 millilitres water for thick coconut milk.

Wash sago well and leave in 1 litre water to soak for a few minutes. Put over heat to simmer gently, stirring until mixture is clear and thick. Add coconut milk and ½ teaspoon salt and continue to simmer until sago almost resists stirring. Remove and chill in individual cups.

Shave palm sugar into a non-stick saucepan and melt over low heat. Do not chill or it will become too hard to pour. Squeeze the other grated coconut with 250 millilitres water for thick coconut milk. Add ½ teaspoon salt and refrigerate if not using immediately.

To serve, top each individual cup of sago with 2 tablespoons coconut milk and as much palm sugar as desired.

Suggested Extra Topping
Boil 2 or 3 sweet potatoes and dice fine. Add to sago in the last few minutes of cooking or simply add with other ingredients.

Kuih Dada

Cooking time: 16 minutes

Filling
200 g palm sugar
40 millilitres water
100 g sugar
½ coconut, grated without skin
½ teaspoon salt

Skin
½ coconut, grated
300 millilitres water
3 *pandan* (screwpine) leaves
300 g plain flour
1 large egg, lightly beaten
½ teaspoon salt
a few drops food colouring (red, green
 or blue)

Dada Sauce
1 coconut, grated
200 millilitres water
2 teaspoons cornflour mixed with 2
 tablespoons water
½ teaspoon salt

Shave palm sugar into an enamel saucepan, add water and melt over low heat. When completely dissolved, add white sugar and strain to remove grit. Plain sugar counteracts any bitter taste the palm sugar might have. Add grated coconut and salt and stir well. Cook for 10 minutes, stirring all the time.

Squeeze coconut with water for milk. Pound *pandan* leaves and extract juice.

Sift flour into a large bowl and add beaten egg, salt and coconut milk a little at a time. Stir constantly with a wooden spoon to prevent lumps forming and add *pandan* juice. If you find the green too pale, add a few drops of green food colouring. For variation, separate into two batches before adding *pandan* juice and make one green and one red or blue.

Lightly oil a non-stick frying pan (about 20 cm in diameter so you get skins of the same size) and heat over a moderate flame. Lift the pan from heat and pour in 1 tablespoon of the batter. Using the back of a spoon, shape it into a round. Return pan to heat and cook for about 1 minute. Turn over when one side is set and cook the other side for 15 seconds.

Put about 1 tablespoon of coconut filling on each freshly cooked skin and make into rolls. Serve with Dada Sauce (see below) as a dip.

Dada Sauce
Squeeze coconut with water for milk and simmer with all other ingredients over low heat, stirring all the time till it thickens. It should take about 4 minutes.

Pengat Pisang Rajah

Cooking time: 12 minutes

8 ripe bananas (*pisang rajah*)
1 coconut, grated
800 millilitres water
200 g palm sugar, cut into slivers
2 *pandan* (screwpine) leaves, knotted
sugar (add as desired)

Steam bananas with skins on for 5 minutes. Cut steamed bananas into diagonal pieces,

about 2 cm thick. Squeeze grated coconut with water for milk.

Bring coconut milk to a boil and put in palm sugar to dissolve over low heat. Add knotted *pandan* leaves and steamed bananas and simmer for 5 minutes. Taste for sweetness and add white sugar to adjust. Serve chilled or hot.

OPPOSITE: Left to right, Agar-agar Santan (recipe p. 158) and Kuih Pisang (recipe p. 151).

Kuih Jongkong

Cooking time: 30 minutes

200 g glutinous rice flour
150 millilitres water
1 tablespoon plain flour
1 teaspoon *tepung hoenkwe* (green bean flour)
1 teaspoon salt
2 tablespoons sugar
2 coconuts, grated
800 millilitres water
200 g palm sugar
3 *pandan* (screwpine) leaves, knotted
30 pieces banana leaf, each 20 × 15 cm, washed and scalded lightly
30 pieces banana leaf, each 16 × 6 cm, washed and scalded lightly
strong cocktail or *lidi* sticks for securing Jongkong parcels

Mix glutinous rice flour with 150 millilitres water until it becomes a firm paste known as wet rice flour. You should get 350 g. In a basin, mix wet rice flour with plain flour, green bean flour, salt and sugar and leave aside.

Squeeze grated coconut with 800 millilitres water for coconut milk. Mix half this milk with flour mixture. Blend till smooth and set aside. Grate palm sugar and set aside.

In a thick-bottomed saucepan, heat remaining coconut milk with knotted *pandan* leaves for 3 minutes. Remove from heat and pour into flour mixture, stirring well. Return mixture to heat and stir constantly till it turns thick and resembles a white paste. Remove and set aside.

Wrapping and Steaming
Put 2 tablespoons of the paste on a large piece of banana leaf. Put a few shreds of palm sugar on each scoop of paste. Put another 2 tablespoons of paste on top of this, sandwiching the sugar. If you like a more fragrant Jongkong, top this with a small square of *pandan* leaf. Fold as shown in the diagram by using a smaller piece of banana leaf across the larger piece and securing with a stick. Steam Jongkong bundles for 15 minutes and serve chilled.

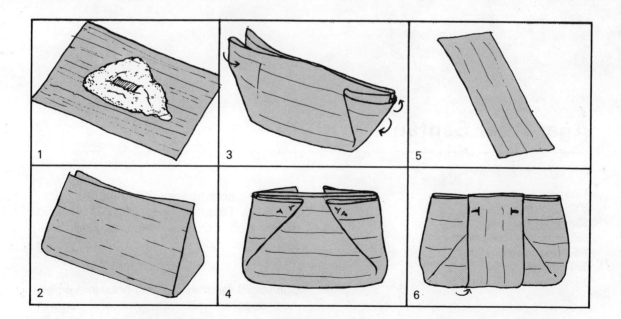

PAGE 154: Top, Kuih Lapis (recipe p. 150). Bottom, Kuih Bengka Ubi Kayu (recipe p. 158).
PAGE 155: Pulot Serikaya (recipe p. 160). Top right, Steamed Serikaya (recipe p. 159).
OPPOSITE: Left to right, Green Beans in Coconut Milk (recipe p. 149) and Pulot Hitam (recipe p. 148).

Kuih Bengka Ubi Kayu

(Illustrated on p. 154)

Cooking time: 1½ hours

1 kg tapioca
400 g coconut, grated without skin
150 millilitres water
400 g brown sugar
1 teaspoon salt
4 tablespoons butter

Peel tapioca into manageable pieces and use a food processor to grate it fine. Sometimes, coconut sellers in the market will do this for you for a small price. Let grated tapioca stand in a deep colander over a dish and remove liquid when it seeps out: for 1 kg tapioca, you should remove about 150 millilitres tapioca juice. This will prevent the finished cake from being mushy.

Squeeze coconut with water for milk. Mix grated tapioca with coconut milk, sugar and salt. The consistency should be like thick batter. Taste the raw mixture for sweetness and adjust.

Dot a baking tray liberally all over with butter, pour in tapioca mixture and bake in a medium oven (gas mark 4) for 45 minutes. Lower heat by half and continue baking for another 45 minutes, dotting the top with the rest of the butter. If top of Kuih Bengka browns too fast, cover with a sheet of foil. Remove to cool before cutting into slices.

Agar-Agar Santan

(Illustrated on p. 153)

Cooking time: 25 minutes

1 coconut, grated
200 millilitres water
40 g agar powder
150 millilitres cold water
1.5 litres water
350 g sugar
3 *pandan* (screwpine) leaves

Squeeze coconut with 200 millilitres water for milk. Dissolve agar powder in cold water. Boil 1.5 litres water and add dissolved agar. Add sugar and knotted *pandan* leaves.

Boil for 20 minutes, stirring once in a while. Add coconut milk, stir well and remove from heat immediately. Pour into jelly moulds and leave to cool. When cooled to room temperature, refrigerate. Never leave hot agar to cool in the refrigerator.

Steamed Serikaya

(Illustrated on p. 155)

Cooking time: 4–5 hours

A delicious breakfast spread over bread or cooked glutinous rice, there is no commercial product quite like it. It is one of the simplest things to make, using as it does only three ingredients, but sad to say, few people can be bothered to watch over the fire over a period of anything up to five hours, depending on the type of steamer you use. Still, when you do make a batch it lasts a long time if kept refrigerated.

There are several traditions attached to this kaya *as it is more popularly known. For instance, when I was about to use the family double boiler to steam one lot, my Cantonese mother-in-law, who learnt it from her Nonya mother-in-law, tried her hardest to convince me it would not be right unless steamed in a tiffin carrier over a larger pot of boiling water. Apparently, it had something to do with steaming it in an enamel container, or was it because the tiffin carrier had handles with which one could lift out the* kaya *after steaming with relative ease? Still, my mother's double boiler was, and still is, as trusty as any tiffin-carrier. This Steamed Serikaya is not to be confused with the* serikaya *topping for Pulot Serikaya. Both are egg custards but flour is added to the latter.*

10 eggs, at room temperature
550 g sugar
1 large coconut, grated (use 1½ coconuts for richer *kaya*)
2 *pandan* (screwpine) leaves

Break eggs into a bowl and stir in sugar. Continue stirring until sugar is well incorporated. Sieve through coarse muslin or a fine wire sieve so you won't get little lumps of egg white after *kaya* is steamed. (My mother always had an old voile *kebaya* in the kitchen drawer for this purpose and I can really recommend it.) Sieving the mixture makes a great difference to the eventual texture of the *kaya*.

Squeeze coconut for milk without adding water. Again, the little square of voile comes in handy here as it is much easier and certainly less messy to extract the milk. Mix coconut milk with sugar and eggs and put in the top container of a double boiler. Wash *pandan* leaves and tie into a knot. Add to mixture.

Fill the lower container of double boiler with water up to the halfway mark. Bring water to a boil and lower heat. Now comes the most important step. For the first 15 minutes or so you must stir the *kaya* mixture constantly with a wooden spoon, preferably until sugar dissolves. Leave to steam over low heat for four hours. Have a kettle of boiling hot water ready to top up the steaming liquid when necessary. When cooked, the *kaya* should be a pale golden colour with a greenish sheen, and crumbly in texture. Nothing like the brown mess we used to get in school tuckshops!

The method I have used is the simplest one. The more complicated one my mother used to employ to make her *kaya* required sieving the *kaya* after it had been cooked for half an hour. She also stirred the mixture constantly for four hours because she had the time to do so. Some swear doing this results in a richer, creamier kaya.

Pulot Serikaya

(Illustrated on p. 155)

Cooking time (base): 25 minutes
Cooking time (topping): 35 minutes

It was a tradition many years ago to streak pulot with blue colouring using dye made from the bunga telang. This is the clitorea ternatea or blue-pea flower, a violet flower found growing wild on hedgerows. It is nearly impossible to find nowadays, but if you must have colouring, use food colouring. Add a few drops of whatever colour you fancy (pulot doesn't have to be blue) by dipping a skewer into colouring and dotting pulot all over. Stir pulot for a streaky effect. While it adds an attractive touch, it doesn't do anything for the taste.

Pulot Base

250 g *pulot* (glutinous rice)
pinch of salt
1 coconut, grated
200 millilitres water
½ teaspoon salt
2 *pandan* (screwpine) leaves, washed and cut into 3 cm pieces
banana leaf

Serikaya Topping

1½ coconuts, grated
400 millilitres water
3 *pandan* (screwpine) leaves
4 eggs
350 g sugar
2 tablespoons plain flour
1½ tablespoons cornflour

Pulot Base

Wash *pulot* and soak for 2 or 3 hours with a pinch of salt. Traditionally, *pulot* is soaked overnight, but this is not really necessary. Squeeze coconut with water for about 400 millilitres milk.

Drain rice and mix well with coconut milk, salt and *pandan* leaves. Put in a *loyang* (steaming tray) to steam for 15 minutes. Streak in colour at this stage. When *pulot* is almost dry, use a clean piece of banana leaf or flat ladle to press it down a little so you get a firm cake of *pulot* instead of a grainy mess. Steam for 10 more minutes.

Serikaya Topping

Squeeze coconut with water for milk. Cut *pandan* leaves into small pieces and pound to extract essence as well as natural green colouring. (Personally, I prefer *serikaya* to be green from this and not from food colouring additive.)

Stir eggs (do not beat) and sugar gently till sugar dissolves completely. Add *pandan* juice. Mix both flours to a smooth paste with a little coconut milk. Stir in remaining coconut milk to egg mixture and then stir in the flour paste. Strain through a fine strainer or sieve.

Combining Base and Topping

Timing is important for combining base and topping so you get a whole cake as it were. Your *kaya* mixture should be ready about 5 minutes before the *pulot* is cooked. Using a fork, prick holes all over *pulot* top (about 1 cm deep) so *kaya* mixture will fuse with it and not slide apart when you slice for service. Pour in *kaya*.

Cover top of steaming tray with a piece of foil and steam for about 30 minutes. Test for doneness by inserting a metal skewer right down through *kaya* layer. If it comes out clean, without grains of raw batter sticking to it, *kaya* is cooked. You will find that steaming with a piece of foil to cover prevents *kaya* from having indentations though some may actually prefer the indentations. It's a matter of taste really. Allow to cool completely before cutting into diamond shapes.

When refrigerating *serikaya*, always wrap with cling foil or the *pulot* will become hard and dry.

Homemade Tau Hwey Chui
(Soybean Milk)

Cooking time: 35 minutes

**200 g soy beans, soaked in water
    overnight**
8 litres water
150 g rock sugar
500 g sugar

Drain soy beans and gently rub off skin. If you leave skin on, soybean milk has a husky flavour that some people do not like. Remove skin and blend beans in an electric blender with some water. Add to remaining water and boil for 5 minutes.

Remove from heat and, when cooled, strain through fine muslin. Put to boil again with rock sugar and half the remaining sugar, adding the rest a little at a time and tasting for sweetness as you go along. Boil for 15–20 minutes longer until all sugar dissolves. Serve hot or ice-cold.

Glossary

Fish Names

Most of the fish sold in Singapore are known either by their Malay names or dialect Chinese names. I hope you will find this glossary useful for it gives the English and Chinese names of some of the more commonly known fish.

MALAY	ENGLISH	CHINESE	
Aruan	Blackfish	鲑鱼	wa yu
Bangus	Milk fish	虱目鱼	shi mu yu
Bawal hitam	Black pomfret	黑鲳鱼	hei chang yu
Bawal putih	White pomfret	白鲳鱼	bai chang yu
Belanak	Mullet	黑鱼	hei yu
Bilis	Anchovy	江鱼仔	jiang yu zai
Cencaru	Hardtail/Torpedo trevally	硬尾鱼	ying wei yu
Cermin	Threadfin trevally		
Gelama	Croaker/Jewfish	黄花鱼	huang hua yu
Jebong/Ayam laut	Leatherjacket/Triggerfish	无腹鳍刺鲀	wu fu qi ci tun
Karang	Spiny lobster	龙虾	lon xia
Kayu/tongkul	Skipjack	飞鱼	fei yu
Kekek	Silver belly/Ponyfish	格格鱼	ge ge yu
Kembong	Mackerel	甘望鱼	gan wang yu
Kepah	Hen clam/Surf clam/Venus shell	蚌	bang
Kerang	Cockle/Blood clam	蛤肉	ge rou

MALAY	ENGLISH	CHINESE	
Kerapu	Garoupa/Grouper	石斑鱼	shi ban yu
Kurau	Threadfin	午鱼	wu yu
Lumi	Bombay duck/Bummalow		
Malong	Conger eel	大海鳗	da hai man
Merah	Red snapper	红鸡鱼	hong ji yu
Parang	Wolf herring/Dorab	西刀鱼	xi dao yu
Pari	Stingray	鲗鱼	pu yu
Selar kuning	Yellowstripe trevally	白肚鱼	bai du yu
Selar papan	Banded scad	竹筴鱼	zhu ce yu
Sembilang/Duri	Catfish	成鱼	cheng yu
Tamban	Sprat/Round herring	丹曼鱼	dan man yu
Tenggiri papan	Spanish mackerel	马驳鱼	ma jiao yu
Terubok	Shad	刺壳鱼	ci ke yu
Tongkul	Frigate mackerel	鲭鱼	qing yu
Udang lobok	Crayfish/Slipper lobster	蝲蛄	la gu
Yu pasir	Dog shark	沙鱼	sha yu

Common Ingredients

ENGLISH	MALAY	CHINESE	
Acrid Tientsin cabbage	Sayur asin/Kiam chye	咸菜	xian cai
Agar	Agar-agar	石花菜	shi hua cai
Aniseed	Jintan manis	茴香子	hui xiang zi
Bamboo shoot	Rebong	笋	sun
Banana flower	Jantong pisang	蕉花	jiao hua
Banana leaf	Daun pisang	蕉叶	jiao ye
Basil	Daun selaseh/ Daun kemangi	罗勒	luo le
Beansprout	Taugeh	豆芽	dou ya

ENGLISH	MALAY	CHINESE	
Bittergourd	Peria	苦瓜	ku gua
Black glutinous rice	Pulot hitam	黑糯米	hei nuo mi
Black pepper / peppercorn	Lada hitam	黑胡椒	hei hu jiao
Black shrimp paste	Petis	黑虾浆	hei xia jiang
Black soy sauce	Kicap hitam	黑酱油	hei jiang you
Brown sugar	Gula timbang hitam	红糖	hong tang
Cabbage	Kobis	卷心菜	juan xin cai
Candlenut	Buah keras		
Cardamom	Buah pelaga	小豆蔻	xiao duo kou
Carrot	Lobak merah	胡萝卜	hu luo bo
Cashew nut	Biji gajus	腰果	yao guo
Cauliflower	Bunga kobis	菜花	cai hua
Celery	Selderi	芹菜	qin cai
Chestnut	Buah berangan	栗子	li zi
Chinese chive	Kucai	韭菜	jiu cai
Chinese parsley	Pasli	欧芹	ou qin
Chinese red dates	Korma Cina	红枣	hong zao
Cinnamon	Kayu manis	桂皮	gui pi
Cloves	Bunga cengkih	丁香	ding xiang
Coconut	Kelapa	椰子	ye zi
Coriander leaves	Daun ketumbar	芫荽叶	yan sui ye
Cucumber	Timun	黄瓜	huang gua
Cummin	Jintan putih	欧莳萝	ou shi luo
Curry leaf	Daun kari	咖喱叶	ga li ye
Cuttlefish	Sotong	墨鱼	mo yu
Dried chilli	Lada / Cili kering	辣椒干	la jiao gan
Dried cuttlefish	Sotong kering	干墨鱼	gan mo yu

ENGLISH	MALAY	CHINESE	
Dried lily flowers	Bunga pisang	金针	jin zhen
Dried prawns	Udang kering	虾米	xia mi
Dried radish	Caipo	干萝卜	gan luo bo
Dried shrimp paste	Belacan	峇拉煎	ba la jian
Dried soybean cake	Taukwa kering	豆薄	dou bo
Dried tamarind skin	Asam gelugor	阿参皮	a sheng pi
Eggplant	Terung	茄子	qie zi
Fennel	Jintan manis	茴香	hui xiang
Fenugreek	Halba	胡芦巴	hu luo ba
Firm soybean cake	Taukwa	豆干	dou gan
Fish sauce	Kicap ikan	鱼露	yu lu
Five-spice powder	Serbuk lima rempah	五香粉	wu xiang fen
Flat rice noodles	Kway teow	粿条	guo tiao
Fragrant lime leaf	Daun limau purut		
French bean	Kacang buncis	四季豆	si ji dou
Galingale	Lengkuas	高莎草	gao sha cao
Garlic	Bawang putih	大蒜	da suan
Ginger	Halia	姜	jiang
Green chilli	Lada/Cili hijau	青辣椒	qing la jiao
Green mung beans	Kacang hijau	绿豆	lu dou
Green peas	Kacang pis	青豆	qing dou
Green pea flour	Tepung hoenkwe	绿豆粉	lu dou fen
Indonesian black nuts	Buah keluak		
Kale	Kai lan	芥蓝	gai lan
Kuakchye	Kai choy	芥菜	gai cai
Lady's fingers	Bendi	羊角豆	yang jiao dou
Laksa leaves	Daun kesom	拉沙叶	la sha ye
Leeks	Daun bawang Cina	蒜	suan

ENGLISH	MALAY	CHINESE	
Lemon	Limau	柠檬	ning meng
Lemon grass	Serai	香茅	xiang mao
Light soy sauce	Kicap putih	酱油	jiang you
Lime	Limau kesturi	酸柑	suan gan
Long bean	Kacang panjang	长豆	chang dou
Long Chinese cabbage	Kobis Cina	长白菜	chang bai cai
Lotus seed	Buah teratai	莲子	lian zi
Macaroni	Makroni	通心粉	tong xin fen
Mustard greens	Sawi	菜心	cai xin
Mustard seed	Biji sawi	芥菜子	jie cai zi
Onion	Bawang besar	洋葱	yang cong
Oyster sauce	Kicap tiram	蚝油	hao you
Palm sugar	Gula Melaka	棕榈糖	zong lu tang
Peanut brittle	Bipang kacang	松脆花生	song cui hua sheng
Petai pods	Buah petai		
Potato	Ubi kentang	马铃薯	ma ling shu
Preserved soy beans	Taucheo	豆酱	dou jiang
Preserved soybean cake	Tempe		
Quail's eggs	Telur burung puyuh	鹌鹑蛋	an chun dan
Radish	Lobak putih	萝卜	luo bo
Red beans	Kacang merah	红豆	hong dou
Red chilli	Lada / Cili merah	红辣椒	hong la jiao
Rice vermicelli	Meehoon	米粉	mi fen
Rock salt	Garam kasar	粗盐	cu yan
Saltfish	Ikan asin	咸鱼	xian yu
Screwpine leaf	Daun pandan	香兰叶	xiang lan ye
Sesame oil	Minyak bijan	芝麻油	zhi ma you
Sesame seed	Bijan	芝麻	zhi ma

ENGLISH	MALAY	CHINESE	
Shallot	Bawang merah	青葱	qing cong
Soft soybean cake	Tahu	豆腐	dou fu
Soybean skin	Kulit tahu	豆皮	dou pi
Soybean sticks (Cantonese: tim chok)	Tahu kering	腐竹	fu zhu
Sour starfruit	Belimbing buloh	酸杨桃	suan yang tao
Spinach	Bayam	菠菜	bo cai
Spring onion	Daun bawang	葱	cong
Spring roll skin	Kulit popiah	春卷皮	chun juan pi
Sweet potato	Ubi keledek	甘薯	gan shu
Tamarind	Asam	阿参	a shen
Tapioca	Ubi kayu	木薯	mu shu
Tomato	Tomato	蕃茄	fan qie
Transparent noodles	Tanghoon	冬粉	dong fen
Turmeric leaves	Daun kunyit	姜叶	jiang ye
Vegetable marrow	Labu Cina	角瓜	jiao gua
Vinegar	Cuka	醋	chu
Water chestnut	Sengkuang Cina	马蹄	ma ti
Water convolvulus	Kangkung	蕹菜	weng cai
Watercress	Pengaga	西洋菜	xi yang cai
White glutinous rice	Pulot	白糯米	bai nuo mi
White pepper or peppercorns	Lada putih	白胡椒	bai hu jiao
Wild ginger flower (pink)	Bunga siantan	野姜花	ye jiang hua
Winter melon	Labu kundur	西瓜	xi gua
Yam	Keladi	芋头	yu tou
Yam bean	Sengkuang	沙葛	sha ge
Yellow noodles	Mee	面	mian
Young ginger	Halia muda	青姜	qing jiang

Curriculum Vitae

Terry Tan, born at the start of the Japanese occupation in Singapore, is third generation Peranakan – his parents and grandparents were born in Singapore – and attributes his culinary skills to his mother. At an age when other boys would be preoccupied with toys, he was already wielding a ladle and beating eggs. There were good times and hard times after the war but the preparation and eating of meals were central to family activity. His was an extended family where there was never any shortage of willing hands to help in the large kitchen. He learnt more skills from aunts and uncles who could all cook some speciality or other. At the age of 15 he was already the family cook but always with his mother's beady eye on him. Being one of three brothers and with sisters all married, he had to cook or he did not eat. And after his father died the family had to keep alive by renting out rooms in their house to bachelors who ate in. But in cooking, he also learnt.

The recipes in this book have been collected over 25 years, and tried and tested for just as long. While Terry has an abiding passion for food, he also had a passion for keeping fit, jogging and swimming fiercely every other day so he could 'gorge' on all the lovely food available in Singapore. Now a lecturer in Oriental Cooking in London, and far removed from Singapore's gourmet temptations, he spends all his time innovating and experimenting with new ingredients in order to continue enjoying his favourite Straits Chinese meals. Terry is married to Dorothy Tan, a former Singapore Broadcasting Corporation newsreader, and they have a son. He loves nothing more than to cook for them.

Index

Agar-agar santan 158
Almonds 14
Anchovy
    Steamed ikan bilis 45
    Fried ikan bilis with peanuts in chilli 107
Angled loofah
    Angled loofah, carrot and egg omelette 88

Babi pong teh 58
Bak kng 137
Bamboo shoot 14
    Chicken and bamboo shoot curry 77
    Pig's lungs fried with bamboo shoots 69
    Rebong lemak with pork ribs 68
Banana
    Kuih pisang 151
    Pengat pisang rajah 152
Bawal hitam 36, 38
Beef
    Beef rendang 70
    Beef satay 72
    Fried minced beef with kiam chye and tomato 71
    Hot beef curry 71
Bilis 45, 107
Bittergourd
    Lemak bittergourd stuffed with minced pork 56
Brinjal 87
    Brinjals with sambal udang kering 90
Buah jering 86
Buah keluak 14
    Pork ribs with buah keluak 70
Buah keras 14
Buah petai 86

Cabbage 86
    Fried bee hoon with cabbage 119
Candlenuts 14
Carrot
    Angled loofah, carrot and egg omelette 88
Catfish
    Sembilang masak pedas 38
Chicken
    Ayam bakar with chilli 75
    Ayam lemak putih 76
    Chicken and bamboo shoot curry 77
    Chicken and macaroni soup 127
    Chicken curry 79
    Chicken in soy sauce 141
    Chicken kurmah 77
    Chicken liver with pineapple 79

Chicken, mushroom and quail's egg soup 139
    Chicken tempera 78
    Deep-fried chicken 74
    Fried chicken with ginger and pepper 76
    Grilled spiced spring chicken 75
    Nasi biryani with chicken 124
    Roast chicken in coconut milk 78
    Spicy fried chicken 79
    Stewed chicken wings 142
    Sweetcorn and chicken soup 141
    Terry's chicken stew 137
    Winter melon soup with chicken 140
Chilli padi
    Chilli padi sauce with lime 106
Chin char loke 86
    Sambal babi with chin char loke 110
Chinese chives
    Koo chye flowers with taukwa 92
Clay pot
    Saltfish rice in clay pot 140
Coconut
    Grated coconut and steamed tapioca with sugar 145
    Green beans in coconut milk 149
    Sambal serondeng 108
    Tapioca squares in grated coconut 146
Coconut milk 15
Courgettes 87
Crab
    Bakwan kepeting 50
    Crabs fried with taucheo and chilli 51
    Kepeting bakar 50
Cucumber
    Cucumber and egg drop soup 127
    Cucumber pickle 99
    Pork, cucumber and egg drop soup 55
    Pork skin and cucumber sambal 111
Curry powder 15
Cuttlefish
    Sotong goreng chilli 51
    Stuffed cuttlefish soup 126
Cuttlefish, dried
    Radish and dried cuttlefish soup 128
Cuttlefish, pickled 87

Daun limau purut 15
Dried prawns, pounded 86
Duck
    Braised duck with chestnuts, dried oysters and liver
        stuffing 143
    Itek sio 80
    Kiam chye soup with duck 131

Ear shell
    Siput lemak   52
Egg
    Angled loofah, carrot and egg omelette   88
    Chicken, mushroom and quail's egg soup   139
    Cucumber and egg drop soup   127
    Egg and kiam chye omelette   90
    Sambal telur   100
    Sweet noodles with hardboiled eggs   121
    Telur goreng   110

Fish
    Fish head and bee hoon soup   144
    See Anchovy, Catfish, Gizzard shad, Grouper,
        Leatherjacket, Pomfret, Ray fish, Red snapper,
        Shark, Silver belly, Spanish mackerel, Sprat,
        Threadfin, Wolf herring
Fish curry powder   15

Garoupa   39
Ginger   16
    Sweet potato and ginger dessert   150
Gizzard shad
    Fish in tamarind and soy sauce   26
Glutinous rice
    Kuih jongkong   157
    Kuih wajek   148
    Pulot hitam   147
Green beans
    Green beans in coconut milk   149
Grouper
    Sweet-sour garoupa   39

Horn shell
    Siput lemak   52
Hum yu fun   140

Ikan merah   28, 45
Itek sio   80
Itek tim   131

Jackfruit curry   89
Jantong pisang   95
Jebong   27
Jelly
    Agar-agar santan   158

Kacang goreng   106
Kekek   36
Kepah   51
Kuih bangkit   146
Kuih bengka ubi kayu   158
Kuih dada   152
Kuih jongkong   157
Kuih keria   149
Kuih lapis   150
Kuih wajek   148
Kuakchye
    Sambal kuakchye   99
Kurau
    28, 33, 40
Kwali (Wok)   16

Lady's fingers   87
    Baby shark curry with lady's fingers   37
    Lady's fingers with prawns sambal   91
    Sambal bendi santan   105

Leatherjacket
    Ikan jebong goreng taucheo   27
Leek
    Leeks fried with prawns   105
Leprous lime, leaf of   15
Lo kai yik   142
Lobster
    Udang lobok goreng taucheo   49
Long bean
    Fried chye poh and long bean sambal   91
    Long beans in dry spices   89
Lor bak   60

Macaroni
    Chicken and macaroni soup   127
Mango
    Mango sambal   108
Meat curry powder   15
Mushroom
    Chicken, mushroom and quail's egg soup   139
Mutton
    Mutton rendang   73

Nangka lemak   89
Noodles
    Bee tai mak soup   129
    Fried Hokkien mee   138
    Hokkien mee soup   139
    Mee goreng Terry   119
    Nonya mee   118
    Sweet noodles with hardboiled eggs   121

Onde onde   147

Pandan leaves   16
Parang   25, 26, 33, 86
Pari   35
Peanuts
    Fried ikan bilis with peanuts in chilli   107
    Roasted peanuts   106
Pengat   147
    Pengat pisang rajah   152
Pestle and mortar   16
Pickles
    Acar   98
    Acar ikan   33
    Cucumber pickle   99
    Saltfish pickle   100
Pineapple
    Chicken liver with pineapple   79
    Pineapple sambal with belacan   107
    Pork with pineapple and green chillies   59
    Sambal nenas   108
Pomfret, black
    Ikan panggang with sambal kicap   36
    Whole pomfret with sambal   38
Popiah   111
Pork
    Babi chin   65
    Babi hong   54
    Deep-fried meatballs in pig's caul   55
    Dry pork curry   67
    Fried asam pork   66
    Fried pepper pork   60
    Fried pork with liver and onions   57
    Hati babi bungkus   55

Lemak bittergourd stuffed with minced pork 56
Lemon pork 66
Minced pork rolls 137
Opor babi 65
Pig's lungs fried with bamboo shoots 69
Pork a la shiok 67
Pork, cucumber and egg drop soup 54
Pork curry 68
Pork ribs with buah keluak 70
Pork skin and cucumber sambal 111
Pork tempera 59
Pork with pineapple and green chillies 59
Pork with taucheo 58
Rebong lemak with pork ribs 68
Sambal babi with chin char loke 110
Sambal goreng babi 66
Satay babi goreng 69
Soybean cakes stuffed with spicy minced pork 56
Spiced roast pork 58
Stewed pork 60
Stewed pork with dried soybean cakes 57
Prawns
 Banana bud sambal with prawns and coconut cream 95
 Crunchy prawn curry 49
 Hot sambal goreng 47
 Lady's fingers with prawns sambal 91
 Leeks fried with prawns 105
 Prawn compote 46
 Prawns stuffed with sambal 48
 Prawns with kangkung 48
 Salt and pepper prawns 47
 Sambal udang belimbing 46
 Udang goreng asam 49
 Udang goreng chilli 47
Prawns, dried
 Brinjals with sambal udang kering 90
 Sambal grago 48
Prawn paste 86
Pudding
 Kuih wajek 148
 Sago pudding with gula melaka 151
Pulot hitam 148
Pulot serikaya 160

Radish
 Radish and dried cuttlefish soup 128
Radish, preserved
 Fried chye poh and long bean sambal 91
 Taukwa goreng chye poh 138
Ray fish
 Fish curry with salted vegetable 35
 Ikan pari masak pedas 109
Red snapper
 Fish moolie 28
 Fish stuffed with turmeric and chilli 45
Rempah 16
Rice
 Fried rice orient 122
 Fried rice Shanghai style 123
 Lontong rice cakes 93
 Nasi biryani with chicken 124
 Nasi goreng Nya Bulat 125
 Nasi lemak 109
 Nasi ulam 123
 Saltfish rice in clay pot 140
Rice vermicelli
 Fish head and bee hoon soup 144
 Fried bee hoon with cabbage 119

Mee siam 120
Mee sua with kidney and liver soup 117
Rojak, Homemade 94

Sago pudding with gula melaka 151
Salad
 Banana bud sambal with prawns and coconut cream 95
 Homemade rojak 94
 Jaganan 87
 Ulam meal 85-87
Salted vegetable
 Egg and kiam chye omelette 90
 Fish curry with salted vegetable 35
 Fried minced beef with kiam chye and tomato 71
 Kiam chye soup with duck 131
Saltfish
 Quick saltfish sambal 99
 Saltfish pickle 100
Sambal belacan 86
Sambal serondeng 108
Screwpine leaves 16
See yeow kai 141
Selangat 26
Sembilang 38
Serikaya, steamed 159
Shark
 Baby shark curry with lady's fingers 37
Silver belly
 Ikan kekek goreng taucheo 36
 Steamed ikan kekek 36
Siput 52
Soup
 Bee tai mak soup 129
 Chap chye soup 130
 Chicken and macaroni soup 127
 Chicken, mushroom and quail's egg soup 139
 Cucumber and egg drop soup 127
 Fish head and bee hoon soup 144
 Hee peow soup 130
 Hokkien mee soup 139
 Kiam chye soup with duck 131
 Mee sua with kidney and liver soup 117
 Pong tauhu soup 128
 Pork, cucumber and egg drop soup 55
 Radish and dried cuttlefish soup 128
 Stuffed cuttlefish soup 126
 Sweetcorn and chicken soup 141
 Tauhu titiek 129
 Winter melon soup with chicken 140
Sour star fruit
 Sambal udang belimbing 46
Soybean cake, dried
 Stewed pork with dried soybean cakes 57
 Yong taufu lemak 97
Soybean cake, firm
 Koo chye flowers with taukwa 92
 Soybean cakes stuffed with spicy minced pork 56
 Taukwa goreng chye poh 138
 Yong taufu lemak 97
Soybean milk 161
Spanish mackerel
 Fried fish with dried prawn sambal 37
 Ikan garam asam 27
 Ikan goreng asam 26
 Ikan kuah lada 35
 Ikan masak asam pekat 39
 Ikan otak-otak 34
 Tenggiri in hot bean paste 40

Spices 16, 22-23
Sprat
    Tamban goreng asam 45
Suk mai yung tong 141
Sweet potato
    Kuih keria 149
    Sweet potato and ginger dessert 150
    Sweet potato balls 147
    Vegetable lemak with sweet potato 93
Sweetcorn and chicken soup 141

Tamban 45
Tapioca
    Grated coconut and steamed tapioca with sugar 145
    Kuih bengka ubi kayu 158
    Tapioca squares in grated coconut 146
Tau hwey chui 161
Tauyu bak with tau pok 57
Teehee char rebong 69
Tenggiri 26, 27, 34, 35, 37, 39, 40
Threadfin
    Hot fish curry 40
Tok panjang 21

Udang lobok 49

Vegetable
    Hot vegetable curry 88
    Lontong 92
    Vegetable lemak with sweet potatoes 93
Venus shell
    Kepah goreng 51

Water convolvulus
    Kangkung lemak 110
    Prawns with kangkung 48
Winter melon soup with chicken 140
Wok (*kwali*) 16
Wolf herring
    Ikan parang asam pedas 33
    Ikan parang tempera 25
    Sambal lengkong 26

Yu tou mai fun 144